CONTEXTUAL WELLBEING

Creating Positive Schools from the Inside Out

D1422244

Dr Helen Street

WISE SOLUTIONS BOOKS

Published by Wise Solutions Pty Ltd
PO Box 634, Subiaco, WA 6904, Australia
+61 (0)8 93888843
enquiries@wisesolutions.com.au

First published by Wise Solutions 2018

Cover design by Neil Porter, Positive Schools
Photograph of Helen Street by Rebecca Carmody
Inside design by Sonya Murphy

ISBN 9780980639711

ISBN 9780980639728 (eBook)

Street, Helen Louise
Contextual Wellbeing – Creating Positive Schools from the Inside Out

positiveschools.com.au, contextualwellbeing.com.au

To my dad
An extraordinary man
who ensured I grew up
questioning the world around me,
standing up for what I believe in
and aiming for the stars.

Acknowledgements

The content of this book is grounded in many years of professional development and personal growth. As such, there are many people who deserve acknowledgement for their positive influence, teaching and support.

In particular, I would like to say thank you to my partner in life and in work, Neil Porter. Neil has a rare combination of curiosity, creativity and 'social wisdom'. His ability to 'see' the context around him, and to understand 'what lies beneath' the surfaces we so carefully polish, is second to none. In addition, his belief in me has been my foundation since we first met. It is far easier to be a disrupter when someone has your back.

I would also like to say a special thank you to Janet Blagg, my editor. Janet has patiently and intelligently helped me to express myself more concisely and clearly while always ensuring I stay true to my story. As such, her editing has added enormous value to this book.

Thank you also to Sir Anthony Seldon for his generous spirit and willingness to jump right in with a whole heart and write such a powerful and relevant introduction.

Also, many thanks to all those who generously took the time to read my manuscript, supply such valuable feedback and write such thoughtful, insightful and supportive comments – you have all taught me an immense amount about education, wellbeing and life and confirm for me that change really is afoot ... Thank you to Michael Bernard, George Burns, Michael Carr-Gregg, Maggie Dent, David

Bott, Andrew Fuller, John Hendry, Jared Horvath, David Kolpak, Toni Noble, Justin Robinson, Paula Robinson, Richard Ryan, Sue Roffey, Pasi Sahlberg, Charlie Scudamore and Tracey Spicer.

Finally, a special thank you to Tess, Molly and Lucia; three gorgeous girls who amaze and inspire me every single day.

What the Experts are Saying about Contextual Wellbeing

In *Contextual Wellbeing* Dr Street envisions healthy schools in which children not only learn well, but also live well. She combines wisdom with cutting edge research to describe how teachers and parents can let go of obsessions with outcomes and cultivate an environment that truly nurtures children's engagement, vitality and development. This is a highly needed and humanising message for anyone who cares about education, or about children's wellness, in this pressured age.

Professor Richard M. Ryan, Institute for Positive Psychology and Education, Australian Catholic University; Research Professor in Psychology, University of Rochester

While some people look at class sizes or teacher training, Helen Street looks at wellbeing. It's not rocket science, there are a plethora of studies that link wellbeing to learning. She points out that the mental health of our young people is a crucial component to resuscitating the educational experience of our young. In a 'must-read' book for anyone interested in young people, full of practical, evidence-based advice, she offers a creative and doable solution.

Contextual Wellbeing could well be the book that starts a revolution in the way we think about schools in Australia – I cannot recommend this more highly.

Dr Michael Carr-Gregg, Child & Adolescent Psychologist, Author, Speaker & Parenting Expert

In times of fragmentation and uncertainty we need the clarity of books like this one to carefully sift what works from what does not. This book provides an indispensable guide to creating healthier and more effective schools.

Andrew Fuller, Author, Clinical Psychologist and Family Therapist

In this important book Helen Street explores how can we create a social context that better supports children's learning and wellbeing in school. *Contextual Wellbeing* is a wake-up call to those who suggest that our students should work harder and longer for higher and higher test scores.

This book is a rewarding read for parents, educators and politicians who wish to create more positive schools for the benefit of each and every child.

Professor Pasi Sahlberg, Former Finnish Director General of Education, Finland; Professor of Education Policy, Gonski Institute for Education, UNSW Sydney

As somebody who has been around since the start of the Positive Education 'movement' I encourage all who are involved or interested in the future of education to read from cover to cover Dr Helen Street's thought-provoking and profoundly relevant book, *Contextual Wellbeing*. She challenges conventional practices and asks educators to seriously consider what it means to have a flourishing community for all. More and more schools are desperate to improve student and staff engagement and wellbeing. If a school is hoping for sustained and meaningful wellbeing initiatives, as well as a collaborative approach from within the community, then *Contextual Wellbeing* is an essential read.

Charlie Scudamore, Vice Principal, Geelong Grammar School, Australia

I don't think there's a single educator out there who still believes *intelligence* is an 'all-purpose' competency that can be taught and applied everywhere. Same thing with creativity, critical thinking, and curiosity: we all recognize that these skills are intimately tied to the context in which they are exercised. The same student might demonstrate deep intelligence when fixing an engine in a noisy auto-shop but demonstrate little comprehension when asked about engines on a written exam in a quiet lecture hall.

Why, then, would things like *Mindset, Resilience,* and *Grit* be any different? Like every other skill, these tenets of wellbeing are not isolated competencies we can foster and apply everywhere – they are unique skills relevant to and reliant upon specific contexts.

If we truly want to make a difference in the mental and physical health of our students, we must shift our sights to the larger culture generated by the relationships within our schools. Luckily, Dr Street walks us through this seemingly daunting task and, in very clear language, demonstrates how we can build the social norms that embody the skills we too often pay lip service to. When the ephemeral mists of Mindset, Grit, and Resilience programs fade away, Contextual Wellbeing will still be standing strong.

Dr Jared Cooney Horvath, Director of the Science of Learning Group, University of Melbourne

A life, a community, a world of wellbeing begins with kids – and that begins with education in families and in schools. Helen Street explores the issues and offers a practical, systemic and comprehensive model for ensuring better schools, better kids and a better world.

Contextual Wellbeing *needs* to be the future of education.

Professor George W Burns, Author of *101 Stories for Enhancing Happiness and Well-being*

At last someone is reaching into what really matters. This book and the careful and critical thinking behind it is overwhelmingly encouraging for anyone working in education, anyone engaged in learning and anyone sending their offspring to school.

John Hendry, OAM, Acclaimed Educator and Advocate for Youth Wellbeing in Schools

Dr Helen Street is driven by a deep desire to nurture individual wellbeing in our young people and collective wellbeing in our communities, and she posits that this can be best achieved through creating 'equitable, inclusive and cohesive' school environments. Her argument is compelling, her research is comprehensive and she provides a most helpful model and a wide range of practical examples to help schools in their endeavour of promoting wellbeing. Dr Street's work has influenced me both personally and professionally and I consider her book as foundational reading in Positive Education. If you want to make a positive difference, and if you are happy to be challenged, then this book is a must read.

Justin Robinson, Director, Institute of Positive Education, Geelong Grammar School

Helen has delivered the book on wellbeing in education that had to be written.

I absolutely loved it and wanted to cheer every chapter. With numerous examples, analogies and reference to research, Helen comprehensively confirms my view that the many programs, interventions and thoroughly good ideas that do not take account of process or context are doomed if not to fail, then to have limited and unsustainable impact. And some may actively harm children. The environment is critical.

This book is not always easy reading as Helen often challenges 'sacred cows'. She acknowledges her role as a 'troublemaker' but encourages us to join her in standing up for real change for children, however much this defies the status quo. Wellbeing begins with 'we' and we need to address the context before attempting to change the person. If you are really interested in making a positive difference for young people and their mental health, start here.

Dr Sue Roffey, Honorary Associate Professor at Exeter and Western Sydney Universities, Director Growing Great Schools Worldwide

Contextual Wellbeing is a thoughtful and provocative book that challenges many of the standard practices in education today – such as school homework, competition, rewards – that have become unquestioned norms. This book has rigour and is evidence-based, yet it is written in a chatty, accessible and engaging style that keeps you turning the pages to read more; I highly recommend it to school leaders, policy makers and classroom teachers.

Professor Toni Noble, PhD, Adjunct Professor, Institute of Positive Psychology and Education, Australian Catholic University

Contextual Wellbeing is one of those rare books that will change the way you think about schools. Drawing on a deep understanding of school systems and human sciences, Dr Helen Street helps open our eyes to a perspective on wellbeing that is often unseen; a perspective that just might be the key to flourishing school communities. Harnessing emerging research and leading case studies from around the world, she zooms out from individual wellbeing to explore the 'glue that binds students, staff, and other members of the school community together.'

Through her willingness to challenge conventional thinking, Helen gives us a glimpse into the future of wellbeing in schools and provides a plan of action to help get us there.

David Bott, Associate Director, Institute of Positive Education, Geelong Grammar School

Dr Helen Street has explored deeply the dynamics of creating safe, engaging schools that bring out the best in students and staff. She challenges many norms that have been shown by strong research to be not only unsuccessful, but often harmful and bringing the opposite outcomes to what is eagerly pursued. Dr Street explores what works and how to implement this into our schools by building inclusion and social cohesion by 'doing with' rather than 'doing to' our students, all while building respectful relationships and acknowledging the role of the school social context.

Maggie Dent, Author, educator and resilience specialist

Contextual Wellbeing provides significant evidence for the important role environment plays in wellbeing goals and strategies. Whilst schools place value on their programs and curriculum offered, Dr Helen Street reminds us that we must first understand the context in which these are conveyed. This book is a must read for all schools planning, developing or updating their definition of what wellbeing is in their school.

David Kolpak, Head of Junior Years (Wellbeing and Administration),
St Peter's College, Adelaide

As usual, Helen's knowledge and 'no nonsense' approach has produced a text that is valuable not only to educators, psychologists, parents, and schools but also to the academic community. Her holistic approach incorporating the physical, psychological and social environments together with policy and practices from the inside out, supplies us all with a model of best practice. This book is compulsory reading for anyone interested in education transformation in the 21st century.

Dr Paula Robinson, Managing Director, Positive Psychology Institute

Contextual Wellbeing is a very important read for school leadership and all educational decision-makers, including those working as policy makers and managers in federal and state departments of education. It is especially vital reading for professionals who advocate for positive psychology, positive education and social-emotional learning wellbeing programs.

As Helen Street asserts, these groups largely view student wellbeing through the lens of individual student psychological capacity. Dr Street rightly starts the search for solutions with a broader definition of wellbeing, one which is 'not simply about individual expressions of thoughts, feelings and behaviours; is not an isolated or solitary pursuit.' Drawing on social and educational psychology research, she advocates for school reform which incorporates student connectedness to their school and to relationships, and for teaching methods that do not rely on strategies of obedience, control, competition and hard work.

Dr Street proposes multiple strategies for humanising education by eliminating toxic school practices: a focus on process rather than outcomes (grades, testing); the provision of more unstructured learning time to promote creativity; establishing social cohesiveness between all members of the classroom and school community and involving students in the re-design of learning spaces inside and outside the classroom – all elements of what she calls 'contextual wellbeing'.

Bravo!

Professor Michael E. Bernard, Melbourne Graduate School of Education, University of Melbourne; Emeritus Professor, California State University, Long Beach; Founder, You Can Do It! Education

This book is a must-read for every parent and educator in Australia. Robustly researched and engagingly written, *Contextual Wellbeing* explains, in simple and straightforward steps, how we can improve equity, creativity and cohesion in our schools. Dr Helen Street's warmth, humour and intelligence permeate every page.

A delight to read!

Tracey Spicer, AM, Newsreader and Journalist

We may wish for ultimate world peace built upon utopian societies, yet all too often we struggle to fit our individualised pursuit of a better life into our dream of a better world. As individuals we often search for a single key to success and turn our attentions to self-help rather than social improvement. If we really want to create a better world, rather than a better moment for ourselves, we need to understand and build Contextual Wellbeing. Contextual Wellbeing makes us aware of the socially embedded stories that fool us every day and provides us with an opportunity to create the society that we want and need, at home, at work, and in our schools.

Neil Porter, Co-founder and chair, Positive Schools Initiative, 2018

Contents

CONTENTS

Contextual Wellbeing – An Introduction by Sir Anthony Seldon

I'M PLEASED TO BE writing the introduction to this book by Helen Street because it talks about some of the most important issues facing education today, and tackles head on why, for all the recent changes in schools, they're still very far from the places they can and should be.

Schools across the world are full of teachers and students doing their very best. But that truth shouldn't blind us to the fact that the traditional school model is fundamentally flawed in the limited aspirations it sets for its students, where many leave having their unique gifts unrecognised or squashed, and many more acquire lifelong beliefs which become self-fulfilling about what they can't do rather than what they can.

Schools for decades have been focused on the development of cognitive ability, as measured in exams and tests. All across the world, governments look intently at these test results to assess whether schools are doing a good or a bad job, and to assess the worth of students. This approach means that schools have been developing only a very limited range of each child's ability. Other, wider abilities may remain dormant for life.

Is it surprising that young people are often ill at ease in their own skin, with many disliking school, and feeling rebuffed by it? Or that we are producing young people ill equipped to flourish in family life and in society, or in the human skills that employment is increasingly demanding?

What has gone wrong? The problem can be traced back to our misuse of the word 'intelligence', a problem that dates back more than a century.

In 1912, the University of Breslau in Poland devised 'intelligence quotient' (IQ) tests which, they boasted, would assess the total intelligence of each child, allowing schools to say which children were intelligent compared to others.

But their definition of intelligence was deeply and profoundly restricted.

For one thing, the intelligence that was being measured in their IQ tests, which subsequently influenced testing everywhere, was cognitive intelligence, commonly associated with the left side of the brain. Some young people are extremely skilled at this intelligence, and they have done very well over the last 100 years in these tests, and later in life.

But other young people, who had differing forms of intelligence, were marginalised, belittled and downgraded by the very narrow but all-powerful definition of what constitutes intelligence and human worth.

Not given sufficient emphasis in school were a whole spectrum of other human intelligences. These include social intelligence, which is the ability to relate well to others, and personal intelligence, the ability to conduct a life in accord with one's values. There are other forms of human ability too that have been insufficiently valued, including artistic intelligence, for instance skill at dance, visual art, music, theatre and creative writing. Physical intelligence has been given insufficient weight too, as have moral and spiritual intelligence.

The worst of it is that the traditionally narrow focus of schools on exams and cognitive ability disadvantages those from the least well-off backgrounds, where there is typically less exposure to cultural enrichment at home that reflects societal values, so school becomes the one great opportunity they have to develop these abilities.

Since the early part of this century, a reaction against the narrow, factory model of education has been building. Across the western world as well as across Asia, the realisation has been growing that schools have concentrated far too much merely on the development of the intellect. Not enough weight has been given to the more rounded and holistic development of each child's multiple intelligences, their character, and their wider skills and many gifts, including their well-being and happiness.

This revolution has been given added weight by academic evidence, initially in the United States, sparked by the work of Martin Seligman and the University of Pennsylvania. This new field of positive psychology showed that young people can be taught how to lead more flourishing lives, and how to make decisions more in accord with their wishes. Seligman famously came to Geelong Grammar School more than a decade ago, and helped pioneer the development of positive education in Australian schools, so that we now lead the rest of the world in the application of well-being and positive psychology.

Many in the west believe that the argument has now been won. Hitherto, the dominant belief was that schools could either develop the academic abilities of their students, or they could look after their wellbeing. But not both. The new understanding says that we can do both hand in hand. But young people seem as unhappy and distressed as ever.

This is why Helen Street's book is so important and timely. She is looking at why the wellbeing revolution has not yielded the expected benefits, and how we can best move forward. At the heart of her solution is the argument that we have focused overly on the individual's wellbeing, devoid of social context and relationships.

Her book challenges conventional notions and practice on well-being and how it should be put across in schools. We've won the argument but we're not winning the war of ensuring we give all young people an appropriate sense of self worth and well being, and develop them fully as human beings. Our approach has been too individualistic. Human beings are social creatures and our wellbeing programs and our schools will only flourish, she argues, when we adopt a contextual, whole-school approach.

Sir Anthony Seldon
Vice-Chancellor of the University of Buckingham
Co-founder, Action for Happiness (with Lord Richard Layard)

August 2018

Contextual Wellbeing (noun)
A state of health, happiness and positive engagement
[in learning] that arises from membership of an equitable,
inclusive and cohesive [school] environment
Dr Helen Street, 2016

Imagine ...
... a system of teaching and learning
where all children are allowed to be gifted,
self-determined and free.
A system where everyone matters,
because the system is just.

CHAPTER ONE

The Social Side of Wellbeing

'Flourishing' is an interplay between our best individual selves and our best environment. This means happiness and success are far more than individual pursuits, or even individual responsibilities. Rather, lasting happiness develops when we form healthy connections in a social context that supports and nurtures us to become the best we can be.

IF WE ARE TO help young people attain a love of learning and flourish at school, then we need to explicitly support their wellbeing. There are various understandings of what 'wellbeing' is, and in this chapter, I would like to introduce a definition that underpins an alternative way of supporting young people, and an alternative way of delivering education.

All too often we try to help a child who is distressed at school by encouraging them to change or to develop as an individual. We want them to be more confident, more resilient, less anxious. But what if the answer is *not* about trying to help that individual to change, in whatever capacity? What if the answer is more about creating a healthier environment for that individual? → home ?

I believe that flourishing in life is an interplay between our best individual self and our best environment. As such, happiness and success are far more than individual pursuits, or even individual responsibilities. Lasting happiness develops from the ongoing creation of healthy connections to others and to the world around us.

Happiness is a positive state of wellbeing resulting from our connection to a social environment that supports and nurtures us to become the best we can be.

The Heart Sutra can be interpreted in many ways. I believe it provides a poetic description of how the spaces around us (i.e. the social environment) define us as much as they are defined by us.

The Heart Sutra
Translation by the Nalanda Translation Committee
Form is emptiness;
emptiness also is form.
Emptiness is no other than form;
form is no other than emptiness.

It could be said that we are living in 'emotional times', with our focus so largely on finding the happiness we want. Hundreds, if not thousands of popular self-help books try to tell us how to help our children acquire the skills and knowledge for happy and successful living. But is this current focus on happiness a good thing? As my mother puts it, 'In my day we just sort of got on with life, we knew if things were going OK, and we knew when they weren't … now it seems that we are encouraged to spend so much time submerging ourselves in our feelings. I am really not sure that is of any benefit … for anyone's children.'

Here lies the dilemma. Like my mother, I question whether this indiscriminate pursuit of happiness is in danger of diminishing the very quality of our day-to-day existence. Yet, with so many adults and young people living in mental and emotional turmoil, the idea of *not* focusing our attention on the active pursuit of happiness also seems an incredibly bad idea.

It seems that we need to do 'something' to help the young people in our care, yet what that 'something' is, remains confused and uncertain. Do we continue to spend time actively teaching the art of happiness to our children, albeit in a new improved program? Or, might we be better off simply encouraging them to engage in a rich and busy life?

To address these conundrums, it is time to look more closely at what wellbeing and happiness are, and how they relate to each other. If we can better and more comprehensively understand wellbeing, we will have a far greater chance of helping ourselves and our children to think about it effectively, or indeed, not think about it so much. Moreover, we may be far better equipped to achieve lasting wellbeing in a meaningful and sustainable way.

So, what are these elusive goals of happiness and wellbeing we all so want to achieve? Is happiness an ongoing state of mind? Is wellbeing a set of optimum behaviours? Does happiness stem from life success, or perhaps something more?

I am guessing that you could easily come up with a basic definition of wellbeing, at least in terms of what works for you. I am also guessing that this definition could quickly become confused or contrary, the more you think about it. At the most general of levels, we all know that wellbeing is something to do with embracing life proactively, but we are aware too that it is also about the acceptance of things we can't control. Many motivational books suggest that our best foot forward is a creative and self-determined one. Yet just as many books are telling us to slow down from the relentless pursuit of our goals and live life more in the moment. Certainly, trying to come up with a definition of individual wellbeing can quickly seem like a task full of contradictions. At the very least, it is far more than simply feeling or acting in any single way.

I believe that any comprehensive definition of individual wellbeing must include our ability to live well, live happily and to embrace life with passion and purpose. However, it also needs to include our ability to hold sorrow, live productively with grief and find hope in the face of adversity. Our individual wellbeing embraces two sides of every coin of feeling and behaving. 'Feeling happy' is just one side of that coin. True wellbeing lies in our ability to express happiness or sadness, as the situation demands it. Lasting wellbeing is all about ensuring that each coin of our various emotions faces the healthiest way up in any given situation. And therein lies the key: 'any given situation.' Context matters.

In Mexico, on the annual Day of the Dead, people remember and celebrate the lives of those they have loved and lost. It is believed that death comes in three stages. First, we experience physical death; second, we are buried and third, we are forgotten. It is only when we are forgotten that we are truly considered to be dead. This understanding of death emphasises the importance of our identity beyond our physical form. We reside in every aspect of the context in which we live and die. Just as the boundaries of our physical form define us, so we are defined by the space around us. As much as every aspect of our wellbeing resides in our individual form, so too it resides in the spaces between us, within the cultural norms of our environment and within those with whom we connect.

Have you kept hold of a childhood teddy-bear or doll, sensing that it was alive in some capacity? Have you held onto the clothes or treasured possessions of someone you have lost? Do you see reflections of the people you know in their homes, their gardens, their choice of friends? The very essence of who we are extends so much beyond our physical selves. It resides within the context of our lives as much as it resides within our individual selves. In a similar way, the various elements of wellbeing extend beyond the individual self.

In his 2002 book *Authentic Happiness*,[1] Martin Seligman defines individual wellbeing across three domains: positive emotions and our experience of them; engagement with the things we do; and our sense of meaning and contribution to society. Since the publication of *Authentic Happiness*, he added two further domains: healthy relationships and a sense of accomplishment.[2] These five pillars (positive emotion, engagement, relationships, meaning and accomplishment) are captured by the acronym PERMA, and together they form the basis of the academic and clinical domain of positive psychology.

The idea of engagement as a central notion of living and wellbeing is not new. Two thousand years before today's version of positive psychology, Plato described the joy that comes from finding passion and immersion in a task. And in the 1970s, philosopher and mythologist Joseph Campbell suggested that we are often caught in a futile search for 'the meaning of life' when true happiness is about finding a 'connection' with life.[3,4] When something grabs you with passion, he said, you need to grab it right back.

This view is taken up in Mihaly Csikszentmihalyi's 1992 book *Flow*,[5] where he talks about wellbeing as a sense of immersion and engagement with the things we do in life. When we are in 'flow' we are energised and challenged by what we do. We are caught in the moment to such a degree that time stands still, and then we find ourselves surprised at just how much time has passed. When we are in flow, we experience wellbeing as a state of deep satisfaction.

how much do we genuinely allow for in school?

These expressions of wellbeing and happiness recognise how we as individuals operate within and connect with our social context. Definitions of wellbeing that focus too narrowly on individual characteristics are in danger of becoming meaningless theories of everything. Wellbeing is not simply about individual expressions of thoughts, feelings and behaviours; it is not an isolated or solitary pursuit. It is just as much about the connections we form with others, the tasks we pursue and our wider sense of the world.

Wellbeing concerns our 'being well' as social beings, not just human beings. It is about creating and reacting to a social context in a healthy and positive way. Ultimately, lasting wellbeing and happiness have far less to do with any aspect of our individual functioning than we might like to think, and far more to do with the spaces between us.

This expanded definition of wellbeing suggests that if we are truly to help young people, and indeed ourselves, to feel happy and live happily, we need to pay attention to the social systems in which we live and learn, as much as we need to support our individual development. We need to look in the spaces between us, between the things we do, between the places in which we exist. Wellbeing is about the space between us as much as it is about us. Happiness then becomes an appropriate response to a positive space, just as sadness is an appropriate response to a negative space.

I have become convinced that my mother was right: it is all too easy to waste time focusing on the individual pursuit of happiness. We may be wasting our time and resources attempting to teach children to be well if, concurrently, we do not also work at creating, challenging and changing the health and functioning of the contexts in which we live and grow.

In the movie *Bladerunner*, based on Philip K Dick's science fiction masterpiece, *Do Androids Dream of Electric Sheep*,[6] Harrison Ford plays police specialist Rick Deckard, whose mission is to hunt down genetically manufactured beings called replicants. The replicants appear physically identical to humans, but they lack human emotions and possess dangerously superior physical strength and agility.

In the book, the heart of the story begins when Rick's despondent wife Iran rejects the chance to improve her mood with a quick fix of 'Penfield Mood Organ'. This device is a futuristic happiness-creating machine. You simply identify the desired state in which you would like to spend your day, dial the allotted number and, hey presto, you are filled with as much 'happiness' as you choose.

Rick embraces the machine to get through his day with what he calls a positive mindset. He routinely chooses to dial 481 which gives him an instant sense of hope and an 'awareness of the manifold possibilities open to him in the future.'

Iran is not a fan of her husband's pleasure-seeking choices, and dials numbers that can leave her feeling depressed or despondent. She even chooses to experience 'despair' twice a month. When challenged on her negative choices, Iran says she believes it is healthier to experience emotions that fit with the context in which you live – in her case, a toxic and turbulent future world – rather than a happiness that is incongruent with this environment.

Arguably, our ability to respond to our environment in a sympathetic way defines the very core of our humanity. Although the mood machine is not mentioned beyond the opening of the book, Dick goes on to discuss the distinctly human quality of empathy as a distinguishing factor between humans and his artificially intelligent replicants and asks us to consider whether we can be truly human if we are unable to relate to our environment. In the same way, I ask you to consider if it is possible to truly attain wellbeing in the absence of connections to the context in which you live.

Individually focused wellbeing strategies that take no thought for context appear scarily akin to dialling a number for happiness. They offer an exploration of happiness that is far removed from the despondency, stress and anxiety that more accurately reflects life in an unhealthy context.

In fact, I believe our attempts to understand young people cannot succeed if we do not consider the context in which they spend their school week, every Monday to Friday. Too often, if a student is unmotivated, disengaged and disruptive in the classroom, we ask 'what is wrong with them?' But perhaps, we are frequently asking the wrong question. The student may be demonstrating a perfectly 'well' response to a context that is non-nurturing, unhealthy or unhelpful.

They may be struggling with their academic learning, as many disruptive kids do. Or they may feel they have no autonomy because they are always being told what to do, which is often seen as the only way to achieve order and compliance in the classroom. Alternatively, they may be struggling to belong in a social world from which they are largely excluded. Consider how many teachers choose to send a disruptive child out of the room, rather than bringing them in closer.

It is of little surprise that many high school teachers come to think of the teenagers in their classrooms as exhausting. By the time that most young people get to high school they have come to the bleak realisation that school does not offer the choices, the engagement and the opportunity for success that they'd been led to expect. At least if we expand our definition of wellbeing to include the context around us, then we are in a better position to support a conducive environment in which to educate our increasingly troubled children.

Most children will appear well-adjusted and happy in a context that suits them. I know that my children's behaviour at the beach on a sunny day can be a total pleasure to be around. And anyone can be happy in the right context, if they have the necessary skills and opportunity to connect with that context. Equally, anyone will be unhappy in the wrong context, no matter how many skills and opportunities they may be presented with.

In sum then, while it is a great thing to develop a strong sense of our individual self, we also need to understand that we are social beings, shaped by and shaping our world. We need to see how we fit into the social world around us. In this, theory can be helpful. My all-time favourite theory of living well is Ryan and Deci's self-determination theory (SDT),[7,8] which seeks to understand drive and motivation within a social context. It proposes that a sense of autonomy, a relatedness to others and the things we do, and a sense of competency are all required for the development of self-determination and connection with life. As such, it goes a long way to explaining the inadequacy of the current educational environment in supporting either lasting happiness or a love of learning. Autonomy is severely compromised in a context that encourages compliance and obedience. Relatedness is compromised in a context that supports competition and outcomes over process. Competency is compromised, for all but a few, in a context that reveres high grades and awards.

No emptiness without form, no form without emptiness. No happiness without healthy context, no healthy context without happiness.

CHAPTER TWO

Current Trends in Wellbeing Teaching and Learning

Wellbeing programs and strategies are increasingly popular in schools around the world, yet the majority are proving far less effective than hoped for. In fact many appear to have absolutely no significant impact at all, a finding that reflects the mistake of imposing an outside notion of wellbeing that is not related to the context of the actual school.

THE MAJORITY OF SCHOOL-BASED wellbeing programs have been built on psychological therapies designed for individuals and individual understandings of wellbeing. As such, they have largely failed to overcome the difficulties of changing the behaviour of large groups, such as whole classes and whole school populations. They have embraced wellbeing as an individual pursuit, rather than one that extends into the social context of that individual.

The bottom line is, these programs have generally failed to understand the importance of context in the creation and ongoing development of wellbeing and self-determination. The more successful attempts may aim to embed wellbeing strategies within the whole school environment, but even these have failed to pay significant attention to reforming the whole context into which the strategies are embedded.

In 1983 America's first lady, Nancy Reagan, suggested that young people needed to learn to 'just say no' to alcohol and recreational drugs.[1] Her words were grasped by an American public that had become anxious about government talk of an 'epidemic of illegal drugs' sweeping the nation. And it wasn't just parents who were concerned; Reagan's speech struck a powerful chord with the Californian police department, and they embarked on creating a youth drug and alcohol program to address their concerns.

DARE (Drug Abuse Resistance Education) quickly became one of the most popular school-based health programs ever to hit American schools. The seventeen-week program involved 'trained' members of the local police force teaching high school students about the dangers of substance abuse and related crime. In addition, students role-played saying 'no' in class to the hypothetical offer of alcohol or other tempting drugs. By the mid-1990s DARE was reaching 25 million American students and was also being delivered internationally. Ronald Reagan's 'war on drugs' had instilled a pervasive fear of recreational drugs across America and DARE was offered as the solution. Its very popularity helped fuel belief in the program's importance, and DARE pointed to the program's wide uptake as evidence of its credibility. Glenn Levant, who directed DARE in the early 1990s, told the LA Times in 1993, 'Knocking DARE is like kicking your mother or saying that apple pie doesn't taste good.'[2] Beliefs about the effectiveness of DARE had become so embedded in the American education identity, questioning them would have seemed shamefully un-American.

It wasn't long before a multitude of research projects set out to investigate and document the impact of the program. Much of this research was necessarily longitudinal in nature, and therefore took a while to surface. And here's when the wake-up call finally arrived. Despite its popularity, DARE was repeatedly found to be completely ineffective at reducing harmful substance use and abuse.[3] Yes, that's right, three billion dollars and thousands of human hours later, the majority of long-term research studies found little or no reduction in adolescent smoking, drug abuse or alcohol abuse attributable to participation in the program. The tooth fairy wasn't real.

Many teachers and parents did not want to face the possibility that DARE was not the solution they believed it to be. In the face of disappointing early research findings of the late 1990s, many schools still held onto DARE as the answer to America's teenage drug problem.

The early results, however, were substantiated as subsequent studies provided more evidence. In their book *Nurture Shock*,[4] Bronson and Merryman even reported findings that alcohol abuse had increased in some students following their participation in the program. By 2004, a large-scale analysis by West and O'Neal of eleven of the most robust studies investigating the program's impact concluded that DARE was, at best, an ineffective program.[5] The truth was that for more than two decades teachers, parents and community members America-wide had enthusiastically supported an expensive but ineffective program. Misplaced faith in the validity of popularity ratings ended up costing schools dearly.

The story of DARE exemplifies several important facets of human behaviour and understanding. First, it cautions us not to mistake good intentions for good ideas. When I was a child I had the good intention of cleaning our deep green hall carpet but, rather unfortunately, the bad idea of using bleach to do this. And so it is with many school wellbeing strategies, initiatives and programs. A program that *intends* to increase motivation or mindfulness or resiliency in students is simply not the same as a program that has been actually found to do any of these things in a real-life setting.

Second, the story of DARE reminds us that just because everyone appears to be doing 'something', that is not evidence for that 'something' being an effective strategy. It might be the trend to set project-based homework, or to pay students in gel pens for being good, but that does not mean these strategies are proven ways of supporting effective teaching and learning. All too often bad policies and practices become commonplace for no other reason than the fact they have become commonplace elsewhere. Or, even more worryingly, strategies become ingrained in school culture simply because they had been established in school culture in previous generations.

Finally, the DARE program reminds us about the power of social norms and deep-seated behaviours, and the difficulties of instigating behaviour change. If only nurturing our health and wellbeing really were as simple as repeatedly stating our aims. How slim we would all be if we could lose weight by pinning the phrase 'I don't eat chocolate' to the fridge door. But attitudes, beliefs and behaviours do not change simply because we are told it is a good idea to change them. And they do not change simply because we practise saying no, or for that matter, yes.

In the face of what might be called an unprecedented mental health crisis threatening the lives of young people, parents and educators really do want to do something to better support youth wellbeing. We desperately want to support positive mental health and social and emotional learning in our students, but we must ensure that our desire for intervention is not so overwhelming that it keeps us from examining the process by which we attempt to implement change. We must maintain an objective regard for the laws of social behaviour, not pin our hopes on some magic formula.

Back in the 1970s the self-esteem movement became another classic example of misguided intentions leading to a disaster in school-based wellbeing promotion. Yet, unlike the largely defunct DARE program, the self-esteem movement still lurches dangerously on in schools and colleges world-wide.

The publication of a research paper in the late 1960s on the significance of self-esteem in reducing bullying and promoting academic outcomes caught the attention of schools who shared those goals. So, with the best of intentions, schools attempted to teach self-esteem to their students. And this is the point at which good intentions and good ideas parted company. With nothing else to go on, teachers across America, Australia and Europe began to tell their students that they *were* great in an attempt to make them *feel* great. It was a bit like telling a sad looking person to smile and be happy. I don't know about you but being told to 'put on a happy face' is a sure way to make me feel anything but joyful.

This enormously popular approach to youth mental health did nothing to improve students' self-esteem or any other aspect of their wellbeing. In contrast, the excess of smiley face stickers and 'good jobs' handed out in classrooms worldwide arguably made true positive feedback effectively meaningless, while lowering standards of assessment everywhere. For example, Weissbourd's 'Feel-Good Trap' (1996)[6] explained that, while self-esteem is indeed an important ingredient of wellbeing, the self-esteem movement did little to actually support self-esteem. The failed movement also resulted in growing scepticism about the value of school-based mental health teaching, and a belief that mental health work was best kept to counsellors and clinicians.

Incidentally, the original research linking self-esteem to social behaviour and good grades, conducted by Nathanial Branden in 1969,[7] has now been discredited by several studies that found no significant relationship between self-esteem and academic outcomes or between self-esteem and positive behaviours.

Despite all this, the practices and policies established during this time became ingrained in the majority of school cultures around Australia, the US, and the rest of the developed world. In 2017, as I type this page, millions of children are still receiving stickers, stars and awards simply for having behaved in a socially acceptable way. Kids around the world are being paid with tempting rewards to be physically present, to be kind and to perform academically.

From the early 1990s, school-based interventions were introduced which focused more on the prevention and treatment of mental illness than on the pursuit of wellbeing. This was the result of a growing perception that mental illness was more prevalent in young people than had previously been thought. Many programs, such as the Primary Mental Health Project[8] and the Penn Prevention Program[9] were centred in cognitive-behavioural therapeutic approaches that challenged unhelpful ways of thinking and aimed to help students understand the relationship between their thoughts and their feelings. Students were taught the importance of flexibility and fluidity in their interpretations of life. They learned about perspective and the concept that 'there is no ultimate truth out there'; rather that some ways of looking at life are helpful, others less so.

Cognitive approaches have proved successful in helping individuals with mild to moderate anxiety and depression in clinical settings, and so it seemed a natural progression to apply these techniques to the classroom. However, as with the majority of school-based interventions, these interventions have been found to be far less successful when delivered in real world school settings than when trialled in experimental or therapeutic conditions (Pattison & Lynd-Stevenson, 2001).[10]

Since the turn of the century it has no longer been seen as viable or even sensible to focus mental health interventions purely on vulnerable members of the community, or on high-risk groups. As Richard Layard observed in 2003,[11] and Felicia Huppert in 2004,[12] the largest numbers of vulnerable young people do not come from minority high risk groups. They come from the mentally healthy majority – for the simple fact that the healthy majority are by far the greatest in number. Consequently, school-based wellbeing programs have increasingly been developed with the aim to benefit all students in a school environment.

Whatever their specific objectives, most of these programs are built on the theoretical underpinnings of social and emotional competency and/or positive psychology (the scientific study of wellbeing). They are frequently skills based and, despite targeting *all* students, *individually* focused. They aim to nurture wellbeing with a mix of social and emotional learning and positive education practice (commonly viewed as positive psychology applied to an educational setting).

Programs seeking to develop social and emotional competency tend to focus on skills which aim to develop individual and social awareness, self-management, pro-social behaviours and responsible decision making. Programs aiming to help young people to flourish (to feel well and behave in a positive and community-focused way) generally concentrate on one or more elements of positive psychology (e.g. resiliency, mindfulness, intrinsic motivation, character strengths).

While there is a growing body of support for the ingredients of overall wellbeing, there is much to question about the fitness of wellbeing programs to best foster these ingredients in young people. In 2011, Weare and Nind's comprehensive investigation of 52 reviews and analyses of school-based wellbeing programs[13] found that in the majority of instances, these initiatives had not had the positive impact that had been intended, expected, or needed. Moreover, in 2015, educational psychologist Kathryn Ecclestone concluded that school wellbeing programs were largely a waste of time and resources. Forthcoming research by Ecclestone finds that 'some of these interventions [into youth mental health] actually have negative effects. In general, the research field is fragmented, one-sided, inconclusive and methodologically flawed.'[14] Just as with the failed DARE program, it doesn't matter how great a program's ideals are, they do not necessarily translate into any positive outcome.

Ideals need to be supported within the context in which they are delivered. There is little point in teaching students the importance of mindfulness on Monday mornings, if the students are overscheduled and feeling rushed the rest of the time. Energy spent promoting a 'growth mindset' in your 'wellbeing class' is wasted if for the rest of the week you focus on forthcoming assessments. Equally, the value of trying to make learning 'fun' is greatly diminished if you take away their intrinsic motivation by rewarding students for outcomes. And it is not just the content of the student's day that counteracts program intentions: effectiveness in 'teaching' social and emotional skills of any sort is severely compromised when the teacher is so overloaded with work, they have lost all signs of social and emotional competency themselves.

The implications here raise profound questions about improving wellbeing in schools. If we could create a truly equitable, stimulating and cohesive context for education, would we even 'need' to explicitly teach wellbeing to children? Are wellbeing programs band aids for 'broken' educational contexts? And if they are as ineffectual as the research suggests, shouldn't we be investing our time, attention and finance elsewhere in education?

My sense is that to abandon 'wellbeing teaching' would be to throw out the baby with the bathwater. Although so many programs are less effective than hoped, there remains a strong body of research supporting the use of social emotional learning in schools.[15] Under the right circumstances, in which programs reflect the whole school context and the problems caused by competitive, inequitable education systems, wellbeing programs can offer valuable support to the pursuit of a flourishing life. The more we do to educate healthy individuals, the more likely it is that those individuals will contribute to the creation of a healthy context for everyone.

Felicia Huppert has devoted much of her professional life to the science of wellbeing. After nearly thirty years of study she believes that the two most essential ingredients of wellbeing are mindfulness and compassion, qualities that develop through practice, not just through theory.[16] There is an increasing volume of research data demonstrating that helping students to enhance positive emotions, identify and engage in their passions, create positive relationships, and find meaning in life really does support wellbeing. Not only does a focus on these facets of functioning help students to be well, and to do well socially and emotionally, it helps them to achieve well academically.

The whole school, evidence-based programs of today have come a long way since the failed attempts to bring wellbeing into schools in the 1970s and 1980s. Positive Education – the teaching, living and embedding of current understandings about the ingredients of individual wellbeing to whole school communities – has become increasingly popular around the world.[17] Its effectiveness in contrast to stand-alone strategies and initiatives is coming to light with an increasing amount of research. The more a whole school program is embedded in the school culture the more it has a chance of permeating the real-world context of students' lives.

In a 2003 review of school-based programs, Wells and colleagues identified the importance of context in program effectiveness,[18] while in their 2011 study, Weare and colleagues pointed to the role of the environment.[19] They are effectively talking about the same thing. Their research shows that the most effective programs appear to be those that have the biggest impact on overall school culture and climate. They, and many other researchers, have identified the most effective school programs as those that are universal, aimed at the entire school population and designed to support the whole child across all areas of education. These are the programs that work to shape the school context – the overall tenor of relationships between staff and students; the social norms; the policies and practice and the physical environment – so that together they work to establish the messages of the program in the 'real world' of school life.

Yet – and this is a big yet – the positive impact of these programs is still far less than it is intended to be or could be. An essential ingredient is still missing. And that is the explicit focus on improving the social context of the school that all too often creates a fundamental problem for student wellbeing. Instead, too often, the focus remains on teaching students what *they* must do for their own wellbeing.

The disappointing outcomes also highlight the difficulty of attempting to create positive behaviour change in students when those attempts are extrinsically directed. In general, individuals change their social and psychological behaviour far more readily when they are self-motivated to do so, not because they have been told to do so.

Clinical psychologist George Burns helped thousands of people rediscover and embrace a happier life over the course of his career. I first met George after he called to compliment me on an academic paper I had written about goal setting and motivation. That call resulted in an ardent conversation about our shared professional interests, during which we decided to write a book. *Standing Without Shoes*[20] was published in 2003 with a foreword by His Holiness the Dalai Lama and centred on what was then a novel idea – that one of the most important things we need to do to prevent and alleviate depressive symptoms is to better understand what makes us happy.

As a clinical hypnotherapist, George was also involved in helping people adopt healthier life styles, including giving up smoking. He told me he usually felt highly confident that he could help someone give up smoking if they had chosen to see him of their own free will. In contrast, he had far less success helping someone who had been 'nagged' to pay him a visit by a partner, child, or friend.[21] When we go to a counsellor or therapist on our own volition, we have already made a commitment to change. When someone else wants to 'teach' us to be a better, healthier person, they must first engage us, then persuade us to the point that we are committed to wanting to change, before they can teach us anything at all.

Clearly, we need to follow the exact same process when we want to nurture wellbeing in young people: engage their attention, ensure that they are on board. This means we need to ensure that young people can see the relevance of wellbeing teaching to their daily lives, that they feel autonomy in their learning and that they feel that wellbeing is a real-world possibility. It is only then that we can attempt to teach them all our well-researched strategies and ideas for wellbeing.

Students are most likely to be on board with ideas for increasing their wellbeing if those ideas are in line with their school social context. In general, we all develop attitudes and behaviours that are in line with the social context around us, the people who influence us, the policies and practice that govern us, the physical spaces that reinforce us and the norms that guide us. The DARE program failed because it did not consider the power of social norms suggesting that alcohol and recreational drugs were 'a cool idea'. Similarly, it is no wonder that modern day wellbeing programs are having little impact in contexts that encourage competition, control, the normalisation of stress and the pressure to achieve.

Social norms are a far more powerful predictor of behaviour than mere ideals. A 2009 study by Mercer and colleagues of 947 primary school students[22] found that classroom norms about aggressive behaviour significantly predicted actual reports of aggressive behaviour over time. This means that if students believe that aggression is 'normal' within the reality of classroom life, they are more likely to act aggressively, irrespective of whether they believe that acting aggressively is a positive or negative way to behave. Our desire to belong to a social group results in our adopting the behaviours that we believe are the norm for the group.

In sum, in addition to asking, 'How can we better support young people's mental health and wellbeing in schools?' we need to start asking, 'How can we create a social context that better supports young people's mental health and wellbeing in schools?' The development of a positive school context involves careful consideration of the relationships in the school, the social norms, policies and practices that guide attitudes and behaviour and the physical environment that reflects the school culture. I firmly believe that if we can get the context right, then student wellbeing will start to improve with or without the support of add-on wellbeing programs and initiatives. If we can put educational reform into context, students will have the best chance of flourishing at school and in the rest of their life.

CHAPTER THREE

Instigating Educational Reform

*We need to challenge and change the
context of schools if we really want to make
a positive difference to youth wellbeing
and self-determination. There is no point
in sprinkling wellbeing programs into
unhealthy environments if we really want to
support young people. Rather, it is imperative
that we become active 'trouble makers' intent
on educational reform.*

THE SCHOOL CONTEXT IS made up of the people that comprise the school community, the policies and practices that dictate *ideal* values, attitudes and behaviours; the social norms that drive *actual* values, attitudes and behaviours and the physical space that defines the boundaries of the school. If we are to enhance wellbeing and self-determination in young people, we need to become active 'change makers' intent on structural reform: trouble makers with an ardent desire to revise and improve school contexts so that they properly support the development of young people's life-long wellbeing and love of learning.

As I type these words, nearly a quarter of adolescents around the developed world are struggling with significant mental health issues.[1,2,3] Nearly a quarter! That is a crazily alarming percentage. The 2017 Mission Australia Youth Survey identified mental health as the top area of concern among young Australians.[4] One in seven aged 4 to 11 and one in four aged 16 to 24 reported experiencing a mental health disorder in Australia.

Parents and educators desperately want young people to leave school with both great grades and a sense of wellbeing. They want them to move into adult life with self-determination, motivation, a love of learning and a genuine, ongoing love of life. Sadly, the education system as we know it fails miserably to achieve any of these aims,

33

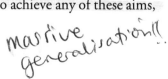

except for great grades for some high achievers. It really is time we acknowledged that this is an unacceptable state of affairs.

Schools and colleges have the perfect opportunity and, arguably, a real duty of care to help young people socially and emotionally, not just academically. Schools may not be wholly responsible for the problems of current times, but they need to be part of the solution. But here's the rub, we are living in a time where *schools have never tried so hard to support young people's mental health, and yet young people's mental health has never been so precarious.*

Today's world, with its focus on happiness and meaning, has seen a broadening of our understanding of what it means to be successful in our careers and in life. Consequently, parents around the world are starting to define 'good' schools not just in terms of academic outcomes and co-curricular opportunities but also in terms of their explicit support of wellbeing: creatively, socially and emotionally.

Schools, therefore, put time, effort and money into teaching students how to 'be happy and healthy' as well as academically successful. However, as we now well know, it is one thing to have great intentions about developing the 'whole child', it is another thing entirely to bring these intentions to fruition, and schools are failing dismally. Just about every school in the developed world has adopted a wellbeing strategy or program, yet in schools I have visited around the world, more and more young people are finishing their final year of high school exhausted, demotivated and distressed.

A mindfulness program may be the new fashion. Or everyone in the staff room is talking about developing character strengths and grit ... but I feel confident in claiming that no tacked-on wellbeing program is going to provide the definitive answer to motivation, engagement, resiliency or mental health in our schools and colleges.

If we really want to turn things around, find an effective better way, we have to turn our attention to what I call Contextual Wellbeing and the development of healthy school contexts.

The school context includes the policies, practices and social norms that guide staff and student behaviour, shape culture and build a sense of community, both in and out of the classroom. It includes the people who make up the school community: the students, the staff and the parents, and their relationships with each other and with the rest of the school community. And it includes the school's physical environment, the physical spaces in which the students live and learn.

Unhealthy school practices abound across the developed world. So much so, it is really of little surprise to see so many young people despondent and struggling. I see primary school kids who are repeatedly required to put their hands on their heads to show they are listening. This means the well-behaved kids are holding up aching arms as others take their time.

I see children of all ages working for stickers and the approval of others, rather than working to improve academic, social and emotional competencies. I see the mountains of homework that high school kids have to carry around in their oversized backpacks. Everywhere I look it seems the school system is run on strategies that promote obedience, control and the need to 'work hard'. In the context of misplaced practices like these, disengagement, distress and a desire to 'escape' the classroom – and sometimes even life – at the earliest chance are all too common. We have to challenge and change the social context of our schools if we are ever to make a significant difference. It is not enough to see wellbeing as some form of band aid add on.

Many of us – school leaders, teachers, parents – are deeply concerned. Yet, very few seem willing to consider that reforming toxic school practices could support student wellbeing far more effectively than any brightly lit program claims to do.

I hear principals speak of the burden on schools to become 'therapy centres' when they are struggling to deliver an overflowing academic curriculum. I hear teachers nervous about being asked to become 'life coaches' when their own lives are overloaded and overwhelmed. I see school leaders desperately shift approaches: from resiliency to growth mindsets, from community to culture, from learning to express gratitude to identifying what is working, seeking the next best thing that will definitively address this problem of enhancing wellbeing. And none of them do. As a timely example, I helped one of my daughters complete her homework on a recent Friday night after she was told it had to be emailed to the teacher by early Saturday morning. Yes, that's right … Saturday morning. The assignment was about identifying character strengths – ironically, this wellbeing 'strategy' was caught up in the unhealthy practice of Friday night project-based homework. A plethora of research suggests that project-based homework does nothing to support learning outcomes and often contributes to stress, overload and a lack of time for social and creative pursuits (e.g., John Hattie, 2014).[5]

When I utter these perceptions to rooms full of concerned teachers and parents, too often I am called a trouble maker. I recently sat at a table preparing myself to present an opening keynote address at a conference on social and emotional learning. A teacher sitting at my table asked me if I got nervous when presenting to large audiences. I do, I told her.

I get nervous because I know I am not prepared to stand there and support the latest wellbeing program without question. I am not willing to agree that the schools are making the best possible job of caring for students in a changing world. Instead, I stand up and create discomfort, unrest; I push for systematic change. This means I am often seen as disruptive, a trouble maker who will not let established practices lie.

It would be so much easier to nod and smile and say what a great job schools are doing with their programs to support their students' wellbeing. And I do know they are trying. But with so many young people so distressed, so disengaged, so unhappy with life, I cannot endorse that path. I firmly believe the time, effort and money could be better spent.

When I stood up to begin my talk, I told my audience that I might come across as a trouble maker, and that their response was a concern to me. I went on to explain, as I had done to the teacher at my table, why it is imperative to be a trouble maker, albeit, I added, a friendly and approachable one. The landscape of traditional western education has become hardened, but it is far from impenetrable, and we have to address ourselves with confidence to the matter of change. I was gratified to be told later that many of the delegates left that event inspired to make waves themselves, to be 'friendly trouble makers' and work for positive changes in their schools.

It is time that all of us concerned adults stood up, despite our fear of rocking the boat, to embrace a deeper, broader understanding of how best to support wellbeing in our schools and colleges. It is time we turned the tables on our current educational environment and created school systems that implicitly, rather than explicitly, support self-determination, a love of learning and a love of life. It is time we developed a better way.

Many teachers continue with the outdated and unhealthy context in our school communities simply because it 'has always been that way'. Others may declare that their classroom-based policies and practices are worth continuing because they get 'good results'. But what does a 'good result' actually mean?

Take a look at the popular practice of encouraging desired behaviours with attractive rewards. A third-grade teacher recently told me she had no interest in abandoning the use of rewards because they 'work really well' for her. (In fact, several studies have found the reward system to be strongly counter-productive to the development of motivated, happy young minds, and we will examine this research shortly.) I tried to explain that rewards work 'really well' to instil a love of rewards in the kids, and to ensure they become more competitive and less engaged in their learning; less intrinsically motivated. At this point she interrupted me to say that she was very happy to see competitiveness flourish in the class, because when students were competing for first place on her reward chart, that meant they were getting the job done.

It didn't seem to matter to this teacher that her students might finish the school year a little less motivated, a little less engaged and a lot more dependent on adult feedback in life. It didn't seem to matter that for every student reaching the top of the reward chart, there were many others who did not. What did matter, was that she was going to get the maximum number of her kids to the end of the year with compliant behaviour, completed coursework and good grades on their report cards. She was confident that her approach to teaching translated into desirable academic outcomes, satisfied parents and an overall sense of success.

I imagine that many of the parents of this teacher's students would feel confident that their children were in good educational hands, in a good school, with a good teacher. I would also expect that many of these same parents would end up feeling frustrated when, at the end of the school year, their kids would rather be anywhere but in their 'great' classroom, doing anything but 'getting a good education'.

Then there is mid-afternoon despondency. Perhaps kids simply grow tired when they have worked hard at their studies. Certainly, this is the common explanation given for the flattened mood of many children in the last few weeks of a busy term. (The same logic would suggest it is a normal thing to end up dead on your feet at the end of the school year, as if this somehow signifies a year well spent.) In my experience, however, being involved in a positive learning experience is invigorating, not draining. I am anything but exhausted if I have been engaged in what I am doing. But, I am totally knocked for six if I am bored or frustrated with a lack of progress and engagement in what I am doing.

These well-intentioned strategies are all too frequently superficial or irrelevant to the actual development of self-determination and wellbeing. They are not embedded in the student's experience of 'real world living' and they ignore one of the biggest problems of modern education – the obsessive focus on outcomes. We cannot nurture a school social system based on competition, control and outcomes and then expect to be able to teach students effectively about collaboration, autonomy and process. Moreover, we should not promote a dysfunctional system that alienates students and then tries to paper over that bleak fact with smiley-face rewards.

CHAPTER FOUR

Creative Learning – When Less is More

Current educational practice stems from an outcome focus, where the pursuit of educational success is viewed as a race to get the highest grades you can. This outcome focus operates on misguided principles suggesting that we learn more if we start earlier, work harder, and work faster. True wellbeing occurs when play and creativity are also prioritised in learning.

THE PURSUIT OF EDUCATIONAL success is often viewed as a race to get the highest grades, as fast as possible. We have come to believe that our kids will achieve the most academically if they get started on numeracy and literacy as early as possible, work as hard as they can throughout their school years, and take repeated tests to gain 'practice' at achieving desirable outcomes.

Most western education systems are based on this outcome focus and suffer badly because of it. In fact, it is a poor road to academic success, which makes it all the more tragic that its continued existence is proving so detrimental to the healthy social and emotional development of young people.

Effective education can far more usefully be viewed as an ongoing process built on a foundation of self-discovery and a connection with learning that is both broad and deep. Schools need to allow young people the time and energy to develop the foundation they need to engage with learning effectively. True education begins with the opportunity to develop self-direction, curiosity, symbolism and passion for learning. In short, *schools need to step back from structured outcome-driven teaching and take free time, play and creativity more seriously.*

Free time is not 'time out from education' – it is a vital path to adult happiness and life success. Wellbeing and self-determination begin within a context that values play in and of itself.

For many people, to embrace the importance of play is a challenge to entrenched thinking. For example, a friend of mine recently invited one of her son's friends for an afterschool play date. Both children are in grade five at their local state primary school. But the friend was unable to accept, for the reason that he was booked in for structured afterschool activities from Monday to Friday, followed by homework, dinner and bed. Another of my friends invited a seven-year-old girl to play with her daughter, also seven. This child too was unable to accept as she was attending a 'high achievers' program that day, a program that offers tutoring in literacy and numeracy out of school time. This seven year old was not experiencing any academic difficulties at school, quite the opposite in fact, she was a very capable girl.

I would hazard a guess that the parents of these busy children believe it is better to be an 'A' grade student than a 'B' grade, and that if their children can be 'A' grade students from the word go, they will be ahead of the game in school, and in life.

Certainly, we can see these parents' reasoning. We reward and honour 'A' grade students in so many different ways, it is understandable if well-intentioned parents have learnt that school is an educational race and consequently want their children to be 'winners' rather than 'losers'. I find it more than a little depressing when schools perpetuate these inequitable, unsupported ideas about life success.

Even more depressing is the fact that children brought up in this ethos are likely to reach the end of high school with no sense of connection to the process of learning. They are more likely to choose a career based on others' notions of status or success, not on any particular passion of their own. A life full of outcome-focused learning leaves scant opportunity to find or develop passions of your own.

These hard-working children are also more likely to reach the end of high school needing the approval of others to feel all right about themselves, feeling driven but despondent and disconnected from their own lives. And when these children fail to get that desirable

'A' grade, they may well experience a sense of failure far beyond that of their less driven peers. A race for success that focuses so single-mindedly on academic pursuits is a 'one horse' race. It can result in social approval but leaves little room for autonomy or self-discovery.

Kids too busy to play appear to be rapidly becoming the norm among the middle-class masses. But even when kids do have free time, they are more likely now to spend it interacting with a screen in a passive, reactive way rather than spending time creatively alone or with friends.

On top of this has come a flurry of books extolling the benefits of introducing academic skills from an early age, a message which is avidly read by parents fearful for their kids' survival in the competitive world around them – fears that are exacerbated by news reports of Australia's 'struggling' academic record. This fear is exemplified in those areas of the UK that still stream kids for entry into high school, where many parents believe that their child cannot gain that golden ticket to the more academic grammar schools without extra tuition. As one parent said to me, 'The only way for them to learn the right stuff to pass the entry exam is to see a specialised tutor out of school hours.'

And in the southern hemisphere, it appears that Asia is rapidly cornering the market in academic achievement. This all too easily leads to the belief that the only chance of success comes with extra tuition. Who will extol the benefits of play?

Parents get all too easily caught up in this race for elusive achievement, and are left feeling inadequate if they bring up their children without extra tutoring and structured activities. It is almost considered neglectful to encourage children to entertain themselves at the weekend or let them simply hang out with their friends.

Yet parents the world over want their children to be happy. The desire of some parents to turn their children into grade-driven workers is typically based on the assumption that happiness comes from

...ic accomplishment, which itself is the result of hard work, competition and practice.

It sounds logical, doesn't it? But in reality, this all-encompassing emphasis on structured and organised activity is far from a recipe for happiness and wellbeing. In fact, it is being found to have detrimental effects on young people's happiness and on their acquisition of life skills.

In an article entitled 'The Test Chinese Schools Still Fail' in the *Wall Street Journal* in December 2010,[1] Chinese education expert Jiang Xueqin observed that, 'the failings of a rote-memorisation system are well known: lack of social and practical skills, absence of self-discipline and imagination, loss of curiosity and passion for learning.' The more we try to adopt China's belief in working so hard to learn academic content, the more we mirror these issues in our children and young adults.

Increasing numbers of studies are identifying significant links between the amount of free time a society allows its children, and the mental health of its young people (e.g. Gray, 2011).[2] Extra schooling and extracurricular activities take away important free time for self-directed behaviour, play and creativity. This equates to greater rates of depression and anxiety in our kids, along with an increasing inability to self-regulate emotions, think creatively, and make self-determined decisions in later life.

Playing to Win

University of Cambridge researcher David Whitebread has written frequently about the detrimental effect of starting formal education too soon. In his 2012 report on the importance of play,[3] he describes the vital role of free play in the development of learning and problem solving, citing studies which show that superior learning and motivation arise from free play as opposed to instructional approaches to learning. He also cites longitudinal studies showing that children obtain better academic, motivational and wellbeing outcomes if they engage in pre-school play-based programs. Similarly, Amita Gupta's 2009 research stresses the centrality of play to healthy child development.[4]

Research is telling us that creativity appears to be declining in children as a result of being exposed to earlier structured approaches to education. This decline in creativity is occurring along with a rise in mental health issues and loss of self-directed engagement in learning. For example, in the UK, educator and author Sir Ken Robinson has reported that creative elaboration (the ability to take an idea and expand on it in an interesting and novel way) is declining significantly.[5,6] This is especially worrying, because creative elaboration is a better predictor of real world achievements than IQ scores or high school grades.

David Whitebread reports research showing that children who start formal literacy studies at age seven (year two) as opposed to age four or five (pre-primary) are more likely to read for pleasure at age eleven and more likely to comprehend the text they are reading.[7,8] There is, in fact, no positive association between reading achievement and school starting age; moreover, those who start formal learning later appear to end up happier, more motivated and more in tune with what they are doing and where they are heading.

It seems that our fears of failure in our developed society have led us into a frenzy of trying to give our kids a head start that is no start at all.

David Whitebread, along with many other play experts, found that kids learn many of the vital ingredients of a successful social, emotional and academic life by simply being left to play and be creative. They learn how to get along with each other – they do not tolerate tantrums in other kids. They learn how to self-regulate and deal with their own emotions and how to engage in their passions. They learn skills for modern day survival and how to foster their creativity.

It should be of little surprise that there is an inverse relationship between time spent playing with others and bullying behaviours. In *Free*

to Learn,[9] Peter Gray describes how traditional hunter-gatherer societies – which encourage endless free play, all the way to late adolescence – experience an almost complete lack of bullying among their children and among their adults. Their kids have learnt how to get along with each other and how to empathise and understand each other.

I am not advocating that we forget formal education and let our kids simply play until adulthood. Rather I do believe that it is vital that we pull in the reins on our expectations of formal structured teaching. Kids, especially young kids, need time for free unstructured social play and unstructured creativity. They need time to be bored and to beat boredom. Time to find a way to engage in life and learn skills for themselves.

The Benefits of Putting Less Time into Structured Teaching

Free time can be found for young children simply by delaying the start of structured education until age seven, as is the case in many educationally successful countries. This doesn't mean that kids don't start school until age seven, but that early school should be about genuine opportunities for play and creativity. We have to stop thinking of the early years of school as an opportunity to enter kids into the race for academic outcomes.

In 2004, Till Roenneberg and colleagues found that teenagers experience a different 24-hour cycle to younger children and adults, which determines that they naturally benefit from waking later in the day.[10] This means that when children reach adolescence, they find it hard to get up for an early school start – not because they are lazy, but because they are wired to start their day later.[11] They are unable to adjust their inner clock to an early start and continually struggle with being overtired. Early rises can be experienced like relentless jet lag to your average teenager. Thus, they benefit enormously from a later start to the day.

Children and young people of all ages benefit from regular 'brain breaks' during class time. Brain breaks are brief physical activities involving collaboration and fun that provide a five-minute break from sitting down and formal learning. The idea was pioneered by Eric Jensen in 2000,[12] and is based on the positive relationship between moving regularly and learning effectively. Jensen found that brain breaks boost circulation and brain activity. Other researchers have found that regular brain breaks increase cognitive functioning, motivation and engagement, and overall academic performance.

In fact, there are so many benefits to taking regular short breaks it seems nonsensical that they are not already a part of everyday practice in every school.

Teachers may protest that they do not have time to 'disrupt the class' with a clapping game or a round of Chinese whispers, but any teacher who has embraced brain breaks will tell you how they have been struck by the positive change in the energy in the classroom. Brain breaks reduce disruptive behaviour and improve the focus and social behaviour of the students. These short and simple opportunities to have fun not only create more time for effective teaching and learning, they improve class engagement and class outcomes. In this way, they also contribute to class cohesion.

Even during more structured class time, an understanding of the dynamics of play and creativity can improve both teaching and learning experiences. An interesting study by Karen McInnes and colleagues in Scotland explored the ingredients of play as perceived by children playing in classroom settings.[13] They found that for an activity to be classified as playful, it required elements of choice and control. This suggests that teachers of children of all ages could make their classes more playful simply by increasing the amount of choice and control the students have over their learning. This could be done as easily as letting primary school students choose the order of morning activities or high school students choose the order of topics covered over the term.

It could mean letting students of all ages have choice and control over seating, or project decisions, or ways of collaborative learning.

Creative teaching involves including students in decisions about how best to find the answers to questions in any given subject area. Taken a step further, creative education encourages students to identify the best questions to ask on any given topic. The more choice and control students have over their learning, the more ownership they will feel and therefore the more motivated and engaged they will be. Their learning will be a positive and creative experience.

Creativity, collaboration, choice and control are vital components of successful academic education, perhaps the most vital components of all.

The Truth about Homework

One of the biggest drains on young people's opportunity for self-determined creativity, choice and control, is homework. Yet, nearly all mainstream schools across the developed world insist on some amount of homework, especially for older kids and teens. Indeed, while primary school children in Australia may receive minimal homework, the majority of high school students receive between one and three hours of homework four or five days a week, every week of the term.

Anyone could be forgiven for thinking that such a mainstream and prevalent practice must be based on a foundation of solid research but, in the case of traditional forms of homework at least, this is simply not so.

There are several great literature reviews on homework, including the 2014 Victorian Department of Education report which provides a great overview of current empirical research.[14] The 130 plus studies reviewed in the report explore the impact of homework on learning outcomes, on parental involvement in children's learning and on nurturing independence in students.

Findings vary, but some definite trends emerge from the data. Overall, there is minimal support for the belief that setting traditional forms of homework for primary school children will improve long-term learning outcomes. It seems that primary school kids are far better off spending any spare time out of school enjoying exercise; after all, kids are very much made to move. It is also essential for young people to have time for self-directed activities and creative projects. Kids of all ages learn and develop autonomy through self-directed pursuits, drawing on and developing choice and control as they go.

Results concerning the benefits of homework for high school students are more diverse. For a start there are more factors to consider, such as the range of subjects studied, the variation in homework approach and content, and the time and effort put into doing the work. Even so, there is a strong tendency across the research indicating the ineffectiveness of homework in improving learning outcomes, particularly project-based homework. There is better support for homework that involves practising skills and strategies learned in class, for instance in maths homework, which has been found to be more effective than homework for other subjects.

Overall, even with the limited support for some high school homework that has been identified in some studies (extremely sketchy compared to the lack of support evinced by so many other studies), it appears that young people spend a lot of time and emotional energy for very questionable benefit.

Certainly, the homework debate is not a new one, with some medical doctors as far back as the 1920s arguing that children were not getting enough fresh air and sunshine due to the demands of homework. For more than a hundred years, there have been many researchers arguing that homework should be banned from schools, or at least reduced.[15]

Many reviews of the literature emphasise the lack of any educational value of homework in primary schools (e.g. Victorian Department of

Education report, 2014).[16] Some published research considers the stress and distress created as parents and children battle each other over tasks and time (e.g. Idit Katz and colleagues, 2012).[17] While many concerned parents clash with their children over neglected assignments, some give in and complete the homework for their resistant loved ones themselves. I am fairly sure that the long-term benefit of repeatedly handing in homework that has been completed by your parents is minimal.

Other studies talk about the lack of equity due to variations in home environments (e.g., Marte Rønning, 2011).[18] The experience of homework is certainly significantly impacted by the social and economic status of families. Some children will take their homework back to educated parents and homes that are filled with learning spaces. Others go home to care for unwell parents or younger siblings or may have parents who are largely absent due to work demands or constraining social issues.

In 2012, the significant impact of social and financial inequality evident in homework outcomes fuelled a major educational debate in France,[19] and President Francois Hollande proposed that homework cease for all primary and middle school students. It appears that a universal homework ban in France did not eventuate at that time. However, the topic was revisited again in 2017 when the new minister for education, Jean-Michel Blanquer, announced a plan to stop homework being done at home to ensure less inequity and reduce stress put on family time.[20] Blanquer put this plan into action with the insistence that all state schools organise after-hours clubs for additional classwork, run by retired or practising teachers or university students.

In 2011 the Los Angeles Unified School District attempted to reduce the contribution of homework to a maximum of 10% of a student's grade.[21] Sadly, at least for the future of Californian school children, public support for homework resulted in this figure being set at 20%.[22]

Some Californian schools have bucked the trend and banned homework altogether, mainly in primary schools, whereas others have increased it and even cancelled morning breaks. Ron Schachter reported in his article 'The End of Recess'[23] that up to 40% of school districts in California had reduced or eliminated recess in order to free more time for academic learning. There is still a very long way to go before educational practice comes into line with current knowledge and understanding.

Of greatest note is Finland's universal educational reform.[24,25,26] Free time now constitutes a significant element of individual growth and learning in all Finnish schools. Homework is generally practice based, rather than project based, and frequently completed at school rather than taken home. In addition, every class must be followed by a 15-minute break, so children can spend time outside on their own activities. School days are also shorter in Finland than in most other developed countries. This means that students have more time for family, creativity, sport and socialising with friends.

The Finnish approach to education has contributed to great academic, social and emotional outcomes for its students,[27] who consistently score near the top in the Program for International Student Assessment (PISA) for reading, mathematics and science. The 2015 PISA results ranked Finland number five in these three areas combined, out of 70 participating countries. Singapore came in at first place, Australia at 14, the UK at 15, and the US trailed behind at 21.

It has been suggested that Finland's impressive results are due to the fact that the language is largely phonically based, so that words are pronounced as they are spelled. This is undoubtedly an advantage when it comes to reading and writing, but a glance at PISA math results alone finds Finland at a healthy 13th place compared to Australia at 25 and the UK at 27, while the US lies at the bottom half of the table at 40th place.[28]

Finland's competitive results have also been attributed to its low rate of child poverty compared with the UK and the US: Finland faces fewer poverty related issues in schools compared to its peers.

Still, having a user-friendly language and financial resources can only get you so far in the pursuit of academic excellence. In fact, Finland lagged behind other countries before the country embraced its radical educational reform, suggesting strongly that it is increased *equity* along with increased creativity and relinquishing competition that have contributed to such positive outcomes.

While its PISA rankings are evidence of academic success, Finland's comprehensive approach to education has led to increased equity for all students. In fact, Finnish educational reform was driven by a desire for equity, not a desire to raise academic outcomes. Unlike other top academic performers, Finland is also reporting high levels of school satisfaction and low levels of student anxiety. In fact, the latest OECD (Organisation for Economic Co-operation and Development) results show that Finnish people report greater levels of satisfaction than the majority of other countries surveyed, coming in at tenth place in a survey of OECD countries in 2016.[29]

There is no denying Finland's phenomenal and highly successful education turnaround. They have become exemplary educational leaders advocating for equity, holistic education and greater freedom for all young people.

I believe that when we think about the value of homework or other forms of structured education, we need to determine not just what is gained from the homework itself, but how it impacts on family and school life. What might the student be doing with their time otherwise?

The opportunity to spend quality family time over shared meals and shared activities is invaluable, as is the time to read a great story to a primary school child, enjoy a family barbecue, or share a coffee with a teenager. More free time also means that children are free to be independently doing other things, without the background stress of looming school tasks. If they are passionate readers, into sport or art, or busy creating any project of worth, reducing homework can only enhance their overall educational experience.

Of course, if your teenage daughter or son would be spending that extra five hours a week on social media or watching reality dating shows, then the idea of time spent on homework suddenly seems a better one. This makes me think that the real issue is not so much whether homework is a good idea or a bad one, but rather, what we consider a good use of a young person's time to be. Homework could be turned to supporting home life, for example asking children to spend time 'helping a parent with chores' or coming up with a 'new topic to be discussed over dinner'. 'Homework' then rightfully becomes about improving life 'at home'.

CHAPTER FIVE

From Competition to Community

Young people have their greatest chance of experiencing wellbeing at school when they learn within a cohesive environment. The development of cohesion is all too often thwarted in schools through an ingrained insistence on competition. Far better to embrace collaboration and a focus on process over outcomes, in learning and in exercise.

IF WE WANT YOUNG people to experience positive and cohesive school communities, we have to create those environments. Cohesion is the social and emotional glue that binds students, staff and other members of the school community together. It consists of meaningful relationships, a sense of belonging, and shared social norms that align with school values and ideals.[1,2]

When we feel part of a healthy, cohesive environment, we are less likely to experience stress and anxiety and more likely to be calm, engaged and open to new experiences. When we experience that sense of shared cohesion, we feel we belong. Humans are social creatures who need to belong. This is not rocket science! It is common sense. Common sense that is supported by very good social science. But a healthy sense of cohesiveness is all too often thwarted within the majority of public and private schools that enforce competition and testing in all areas of school life.

The Finnish Way

Since I began writing this book, I have been continually fascinated to see that my passion for developing a better context for education mirrors much of the successful education reform that has occurred in Finland in recent years. Reform that has resulted in Finnish students achieving enviable academic excellence. When the PISA (Program for International Student Assessment) results of 2001 placed Finland near the top of its scale of academic achievement, other countries noticed. Curiously, the vast majority of these other countries have yet to move with meaningful reform of their own. I fear that our belief in the power of competition and an outcome focus to bring educational success has overridden our openness to positive change.

In the previous chapter we looked at Finland's support of equity, free time, play and creativity for all young people. In addition, the Finns have successfully developed other aspects of school context over the past twenty years. There are no private schools in Finland. All pupils are offered free meals, easy access to health and psychological care and individual support when needed. All teachers are highly skilled, holding at least a master's degree. For the students, there is no streaming, no testing and no grades until the final year of high school. In embracing self-determination for their youth, the Finns have kept competition and stress to a minimum and are now leading the world with the academic excellence, self-determination and wellbeing that the rest of us are looking for.

Perhaps we supporters of positive education have been asking the wrong questions. Rather than, 'How can we improve the wellbeing of young people in our schools?' perhaps we should be asking, 'How can we improve equity, creativity and cohesion?'

Equity, creativity and cohesion are all foundational attributes for global wellbeing. And they are not going to arise by ladling wellbeing programs on top of inequitable, competitive highly structured systems in education.

Outside of Finland, school students around much of the developed world are not only missing out on equity and creative time, they are being taught to strive to win. They quickly learn to compete with their peers for awards, trophies and high grades. They are taught that some kids are 'gifted' and others are most definitely not. They are taught that winners are entitled to public acclaim, and everyone else is second best at most.

Competition is often imposed in schools in the belief that it leads to 'motivation' to work hard and teaches 'resiliency' through exposure to failure. Competition is typically considered to be a 'fun' way to learn and a great way to feel a part of a team.

Certainly, competition has a place in school-based recreational sport and other games. Healthy opportunities for competition can arguably help kids appreciate that achievement comes from effort, and that although failure can be disappointing, it can be survived. After all, failing well is a mark of future success. Healthy competition, where kids can learn to fail in a safe environment, *can* indeed help build resiliency. However, this does not mean that it is appropriate or sensible to make kids compete in every area of their learning, especially where the winning and losing is a foregone conclusion. If we do that, we might be telling kids they are 'all equally valued' at school, but our behaviour shows a very different story.

The Cost of Excellence

Back in 2016, my family became completely caught up in Rio Olympic fever. We revelled in watching the gymnastics, the equestrian events, the rowers. We were delighted and inspired by so many dedicated and talented athletes. The Olympic games would not be the Olympic games if there were no gold medals, no winners, or losers. Those athletes with medals return home jubilant, embracing the celebrations that greet them. However, we know that many of these winners find it hard to adjust to life after the attention following the Olympics has waned. And of course, there can be great disappointment and emotional distress among those who fail to win a medal or don't qualify to even compete.

A good friend of mine, the very reverend Richard Pengelley, competed as a water polo player in two consecutive Olympic games in the 1980s. Now in his mid-fifties, there is no doubt that Richard is a natural athlete. He is also someone who spent much of his adolescence staring at a black line at the bottom of the pool. Richard worked extremely hard in his pursuit of excellence.[3] I recently asked him if he thought that the sacrifices he had made as a teenager, training four hours a day in the pool, were worth it.

He was uncertain. He was fairly sure he couldn't have participated in the Olympics without an incredible amount of hard work and dedication, but did also wonder if life could have been happier, somehow easier in his youth if he had taken a less gritty path. Still, as an adult, he has many treasured accomplishments to look back on.

I wonder how different Richard's answer would have been if he had not made the cut for the Olympic team. He may have felt crushed by a sense of a wasted youth, or equally, he may have felt satisfied that he had given his Olympic dream his best shot. There is just as much risk in *not* putting in 'your all' to achieve a longed-for goal, as in giving your all and then not reaching your goal.

However, unlike at the Olympics, winning at the primary school sports carnival is a lot more about genetics than about personal agency. The kids who win, win because they were born with genes that make them faster, more co-ordinated, and more able to win — not because of years of dedicated training. As such, giving the speediest child in grade one a medal is little different to giving them a prize for having the blondest hair or the bluest eyes. It is a practice of active discrimination that has little to do with supporting passion or perseverance.

Certainly, champion girls and boys generally love the sports carnival. And why wouldn't they? It offers them an opportunity to experience the good feeling of winning, with abundant praise and approval. Generally speaking, the kids that win in grade one are the same kids who win in grades two to six and beyond. They have the best genetics for sport and the motivating adulation of everyone around them. However, just like the Olympic athletes, these school carnival winners may find it hard to deal with coming second, later in life.

By contrast, the kids who come last in grade one generally continue to come last as they compete from year to year. These kids quickly learn that they are not winners in the eyes of the school, in fact they may feel like fodder for the success of their peers. Many will break out in a cold sweat at the thought of sprints and long jumps. They are not enjoying the journey, knowing that winning was never an option. For these kids, the sports field is little short of being fed to the lions. It is understandable that so many give up on sport entirely as soon as they can.

Then there are children who were not necessarily born with a lot of sporting potential, yet they still love to take part. These are the children who have a natural tendency to invest in their journey without fear of the outcome. They can enjoy the atmosphere of the sports carnival, cheer on their peers and feel happy to be part of a team. This is a healthy approach to a social situation and a healthy expression of resiliency and belonging. Sadly, the healthy mindset of some of these young people will be slowly eroded when they learn that it is the outcomes that really matter to the school.

Children internalise the reality of their social context, not the slogans of school mottos. For many schools, the sports carnival is not a celebration of team spirit and 'having a go'. It doesn't matter how much you tell kids 'participation is everything' if it is the same high achievers who repeatedly receive all the attention. Showing is always more powerful than telling.

We need to ensure that competitive sport in schools is healthy and equitable for all. As things stand, the winning kids are failing to learn how to lose, while everyone else is failing to feel like they've won.

Conditional Goal Setting

It is time we acknowledged that forced public competition in schools does little to build resiliency or motivation, and thwarts attempts to create cohesion, community and equity.

In the late 1990s I developed a theory called 'Conditional Goal Setting' (CGS).[4,5] My research, and subsequent research of other academics, has found that individuals who make their wellbeing *conditional* upon achieving a goal are more likely to suffer depression and unhappiness than those whose focus is simply on enjoying the processes of goal pursuit.

Those of us who are conditional goal setters spend a lot of time judging our lives to be unhappy and unsatisfactory. No matter what goal we are working towards, all of us generally spend far more time in the process of goal pursuit than we do at the culmination. So, if we believe that we need to attain a particular goal to be happy, all the time we are pursuing that goal, we are in the condition of being not happy yet. Moreover, if we fail to accomplish our happiness-defining goal altogether, we believe we have lost our chance to be happy. People rarely enjoy the process of goal pursuit, win, or lose, if they invest too much of their wellbeing in the idea of reaching the end of their journey.

Even if conditional goal setters do achieve their aims, most experience only a brief period of elation before they habituate to their success. They then find themselves investing their happiness in the next outcome ... and the next.

Conditional goal setting is seen among the driven but depressed athletes who put everything into reaching their goals and then wonder what their life is all about. It is also seen among high achievers in other domains and many people who seem to constantly seek social success. We see CGS in the single person desperate to be married; the employee longing for promotion and the starving adolescent who believes that being the thinnest means being the most popular.

The praise and prizes repeatedly given to the 'winners' and high achievers in schools encourages CGS and a perpetual outcome focus. Young people of all abilities are being trained to keep their 'eye on the prize' and believe that winning brings joy and belonging, and losing means failure in every sense.

Determined Genes

Angela Duckworth talks about the concept of 'grit'[6] – a combination of passion and perseverance that is currently very popular in schools, probably because it is a significant driver of outcome success in an outcome focused system. Indeed, grit has been frequently observed in high achievers at school. But grit is not necessarily a recipe for success when it comes to life satisfaction and wellbeing.

If you embrace grit and determination, you may reach your goals and feel good. Or … you may not. There is little increase in your wellbeing if you achieve goals with gritted determination but pay no heed to the joys of the journey.

Moreover, as Duckworth admits, grit is not enough on its own to guarantee success. No matter how determined you are, you also require a certain amount of good fortune and natural ability to reach the top of your chosen pursuit. The world of self-help might wish to convince us otherwise, but we don't always 'achieve our dream' simply because we desire it, or even because we work really hard. Ask any gritty contestant who has lost out in auditions for a talent show.

In addition, as positive education expert David Bott stated at the Australian Positive Schools 2017 conference, there is a big difference between 'intelligent grit' and 'stupid grit' when it comes to success.[7] Ten thousand hours of unintelligent practice does not lead to expertise. (I know this from my many, many attempts at parallel parking!) Our purpose and passion need to be combined with awareness of the stage we are at in our journey and a sensible approach to the pursuit of our goals.

If we want young people to have the best chance of experiencing wellbeing and building resiliency, we need to help them identify their strengths, find their passions, learn how to fail and how to succeed, and commit to their journey – their way. Making young people compete in a public arena, irrespective of their strengths or passions, does not allow for all this to happen, even for those who are leading the race.

Thinner, Fatter ... Brighter, Better

In their study of wellbeing, Christopher Peterson and Martin Seligman identified twenty-four different character strengths that we are all capable of expressing, some more so than others.[8] While different character strengths become evident in different people at different times, the growing body of literature on strengths tells us that we each have elements of our character that are particularly salient for us. Your most commonly expressed strengths might include kindness, curiosity, humour or bravery, among many others.

Similarly, it could be said that we all have different mental strengths. Some of us are more naturally mathematical, some have great imaginations. Some of us excel at creative elaboration or art, others have a natural affinity for written language, or are great at building 3D structures. Just as with our character, we can develop our mental skills and abilities with passion and perseverance, but at the same time, our natural predispositions will vary.

We are also incredibly varied in our natural physical abilities, as the school sports carnival shows us, and have varying degrees of natural talent on the football field, in dance, drama and other bodily pursuits. Some of us are taller, stronger, more coordinated than others, not because of grit and determination, but simply because of genetics.

A good education is a well-rounded one. We all want our children to learn numeracy and literacy skills, to be physically active, to demonstrate good values and appropriate social behaviour. Children need the opportunity to find, explore and embrace their most salient character traits, mental predispositions and physical abilities. They need the opportunity to find and build on their natural strengths, to engage in and enjoy the process of learning. They need to learn to fail when there is a real chance of success. They need to be able to do these things in a cohesive, safe, equitable environment.

Those who always win, fear to lose; those who continually lose, fear they will never come first.

Ill thought out mandatory competition can be found everywhere in our school communities. Nowadays we give prizes for effort, never mind academic achievement. Some schools even give out prizes for social and emotional skills. I have seen teachers stop kids in the playground and give them an award for being polite to another child. If a child wins a merit award for being 'kind to her peers' does that mean everyone else is less than kind?

Even in the 'world gone mad' sports carnivals where everyone gets a ribbon, or the merit ceremonies where every child gets a prize for something, the emphasis is still firmly on the goal not the journey. These trophies for everyone fool no-one. Kids know there are still winners out there ... and losers. They know that the naturally (genetically) advantaged minority gain the coveted prizes, and greater social acceptance and public approval than everyone else. It is simply 'not fair' to insist that every child is continually pitted against their peers.

This short-sighted approach to education discourages many kids from 'having a go', simply through fear of losing. Moreover, whether they win or lose, many young children are not ready to 'perform in public'. Social risk-taking needs to be child led, not based on an imposed rule.

It is of little wonder that young people end up competing with each other over their physical beauty or weight. We tell teenagers to accept and love the bodies they have but then we show them a world where there are winners and losers in every arena, and genetics count.

Enforced competition also destroys healthy cohesion. Students feel unsafe and lack trust in each other when they are surrounded by competitors, fighting to survive. Even classrooms provide little time out from constant tests of worth. The teachers may claim that it is the comments that count on the report cards, but in reality, it is the grades that garner parent attention, as students know very well. The Monday morning after reports have gone home, students everywhere, subtly, or blatantly, compare to see who scored the highest; who is 'the best'.

There is no need to give outcome grades or tests to kids who are still learning. There is no need to judge and rank them. Learning is an ongoing process that requires opportunity to engage and have a go at all manner of activities, at an appropriate level of risk, without forced competition. Learning benefits from ongoing constructive feedback and opportunities for growth, not from continuous testing and judgement. And as to ongoing feedback, if the comments matter more than the grades, let's get rid of the grades altogether.

Back in 1988 the world was glued to the Winter Olympics games in Calgary, Canada and they were cheering for a very different sort of star. Michael 'Eddie' Edwards had qualified as a ski jumper for the UK, not because of any outstanding sporting talent but simply because of his determination and grit … and because no-one else had competed. Ski jumping is not a popular choice amid the rolling hills of England.

When it was Eddie's turn to take off from the 70m high jump at the Olympics, he managed a modest 55 metres, putting him in last place on the score board. But Eddie was jubilant. He had fulfilled his dream and he could hardly believe it. Not only had he participated in the Olympic games, he had reached a personal best.

As Eddie cheered and waved his arms, the audience cheered at his enthusiasm. It was as if he had reminded them of something that had almost been forgotten in the world of modern competitive sport: the joy of participation, where success lay in simply having 'done your best'.

Eddie became known as 'Eddie the Eagle' due to his fervent arm waving to the crowd following that first jump. Not wanting to be considered a 'flash in the pan' of Olympic moments, he decided to have a go at the 90m high jump. He had never attempted it before …

As Eddie prepared himself, a watching world held its breath. Again, he managed the jump and landed without injury or fall. Once again, he came last, and once again he was ecstatic, as were the millions who watched him around the world.

When Eddie returned to the UK he was met by joyous crowds. He had no medal to show but his character and spirit had won the hearts of the British public. It was a great reminder of times past when the Olympics was for amateur athletes, competing with good character and good will.

This is what community building events need to offer – opportunities for everyone to participate, according to their different strengths and levels of maturity. Some kids may want to participate in races at the sports carnival, or in a debating challenge or music competition, and that is great. Others may prefer to organise flyers, take photos for the school website, or prepare refreshments. Let's leave the competitive races for those who love to compete.

From the 'A' Class to the Mall

On a cold January morning in 2007 one of the world's most revered classical violinists was invited to participate in a social experiment. *Washington Post* journalist Gene Weingarten had asked Joshua Bell if he would play his violin near the entry of a Washington shopping mall, incognito, while being filmed by hidden cameras.[9]

Joshua had quickly agreed to the idea, intrigued to see what would happen. He arrived early at the shopping mall the morning after performing to a packed and rapturous house at the Boston Symphony Hall, wearing the same style of casual clothes he had worn the night before and carrying the same three million-dollar Stradivari violin. His set included one of the most difficult pieces every written for the violin, Bach's 'Chaconne', and the ever popular 'Ave Maria' by Schubert.

During the forty-three minutes of Joshua's performance, more than a thousand people walked by. More people stood in a near-by queue, waiting to check their lottery tickets, while others worked within view, including a security guard and a shoe shine worker. Only seven of these more than a thousand people stopped for longer than a minute. No-one in the lottery queue even turned around. There was no applause after any piece finished, and Joshua made a total of a little over $32 during his busking adventure. In his normal professional life, he could command more than $1000 a minute.

In the story he wrote for the *Washington Post*, Gene reported that Joshua admitted to feeling nervous before performing and went on to say that when he played in a grand venue, he felt validated before he took to the stage. The shopping mall offered no grandeur, no pre-performance validation, and no certainty of anyone's attention. In particular, Joshua found the deafening silence of no-one applauding very difficult to deal with.

This great experiment illustrates two very important points about the power of context. First, the way context can shape the way others perceive us. The people who heard Joshua play incognito in the shopping mall perceived the value of his performance very differently from those who went to hear him play in the concert hall.

Second, context can shape the way we perceive ourselves. Joshua felt very differently about his performance in the concert hall than he did in the shopping mall. Although he played well in both environments, in the concert hall he felt confident, validated and happy. In the shopping mall he felt unsure, awkward and ultimately a little distressed.

One of the most competitive practices in classrooms and schools is that of streaming, or tracking as it is called in the US. You could say that streaming places kids in different contexts to teach and learn. Kids placed in gifted, advanced or 'A' stream classes are like Joshua performing in the concert hall, while those placed in the learning support, lower or 'D' stream classes are like Joshua playing in the shopping mall.

Kids in the 'A' groups generally perceive themselves to be more competent, more validated, more valued than do their peers. Also, teachers judge kids in 'A' groups to be more competent than kids in lower groups, irrespective of actual ability. These contextually influenced beliefs are so powerful, streaming all too easily becomes a self-fulfilling prophecy.[10,11]

It also becomes very difficult for children to move up (or indeed down) groups. Teachers tend to use the context of existing group allocation as a measure of ability for making decisions about future group allocation. Children too tend to judge their own abilities and potential on the basis of their group allocation, far more than on any other factor. Children's beliefs, thoughts and feelings are heavily shaped by their context, irrespective of what others say about their ability or potential.[12]

Streaming generally begins in the early years of primary school when children are placed in ability groups for reading. Children may not be told that they are being ranked and in fact the groups, which are assigned books that match their reading ability, are often given arbitrary names, like 'possums', 'butterflies' or 'dragons'. In reality, we all know that children are often far more aware than we might like to admit. They quickly work out that their groups are ranked, separating the advanced readers from the least advanced. The 'possums' quickly become the 'concert hall' group and the 'dragons' become the 'mall' buskers.

Research tells us that children are more likely to persevere with reading, and to develop passion for it, if they are reading books with great *content*, rather than books that match their reading ability. Far better that we organise groups on the basis of subject matter rather than difficulty. Reading is, after all, a means to an end, not an end in itself. For young children, it needs to be a means to enjoying great stories and other interesting texts.

Between-class groups – in which children are placed in a particular class according to their ability, as opposed to in-class grouping, where children are grouped according to ability within the same class – are generally designed to be fluid and non-competitive. In reality, the children streamed in between-class groups find it particularly hard to move groups once they have been allocated to a particular stream. Not only are perceptions of their abilities affected by the group in which they are placed, teaching style and content often varies significantly between streams, making it doubly hard to move.

The content taught is generally richer in higher groups, with more time allocated for students to have choice, control and ownership over their learning. This means that students in lower groups are disadvantaged by reduced content and diminished skills. They also lose motivation due to their perceived lower status and also because they have experienced less autonomy, proactive learning and ultimate success. Researchers at the Economic and Social Research Institute in Ireland, Emer Smyth and Selina McCoy, are strongly opposed to ability grouping. In their 2011 review of the literature[13] they suggest that significant numbers of students in lower streams disengage with learning as soon as they realise that their learning opportunities have been dashed.

Things are better for students placed in the higher groups, but still not that great. Teachers tend to assume there is little variance in a class that has been formed on the basis of ability, but this is simply not the case. There is still plenty of variation within each stream, and many kids in higher streams struggle with the pressure of highly challenging work and trying to keep up with their peers.

Of course, there are benefits to being in the higher streams. Like Joshua Bell in the concert hall, 'A' stream students learn that they are valued and have opportunity ahead. But these are benefits experienced by a very small minority of young people within a school, and not necessarily even those with the most potential for academic life.

Certainly, when we consider education as a whole, there is nothing equitable about streaming. And equity is arguably the most vital component of successful education, essential for positive academic outcomes, self-determination and wellbeing.

Just ask the Finns ...

CHAPTER SIX

Motivation, Compliance and Control

A mass of research tells us that reward-based learning demotivates children because they turn their attentions to the reward on offer, rather than to the task at hand. In contrast, intrinsic motivation develops when we support autonomy, positive relations and a focus on the process of learning.

RATHER THAN BEING CONCERNED with how 'much' motivation our children have, we ought to focus on 'what kind': intrinsic or extrinsic.[1] Intrinsic motivation comes from within the process of pursuing a task. For example, we are intrinsically motivated to read a book when we are hooked by the opening chapter. Or we may be intrinsically motivated to catch up with a friend because we enjoy their company.

Intrinsic motivation is concerned with the ongoing pursuit of a task and brings with it connection with the task and persistence in the task. If a task is rewarding in its own right, we want to keep doing it. If we have a job that is intrinsically motivating, we are more likely to enjoy our working life and to want to work. Pay is not necessarily the primary issue for us: we find ourselves working *with* pay, rather than working *for* it. It is of little surprise to find that intrinsic motivation is significantly linked to wellbeing, self-determination and overall engagement in the process of living and learning. After all, wellbeing is about living, connecting and sometimes dancing with life.

Extrinsic motivation, on the other hand, comes from something external to the task we are pursuing, often a reward or anticipated outcome. We may be extrinsically motivated to go to work because we want to get paid. We may be extrinsically motivated to watch a game of football to please someone else. Extrinsic motivation is dependent on the appeal of a particular outcome, irrespective of the task. If the motivating outcome is removed, the task soon becomes unappealing. If we only work because we need the income, we are likely to feel miserable and disconnected in our day to day working life and may be quick to hand in our notice if we could be paid more elsewhere.

Extrinsic motivation leads to a reliance on particular outcomes; it is associated with a lack of engagement in the processes of living, and a focus on getting to the end of each task. So it is of little surprise that relying on extrinsic motivation is linked to poor wellbeing and dissatisfaction. As mindfulness experts point out, we lose wellbeing when we are so busy aiming for the finish line that we forget to pay attention to today.

In the art of education, intrinsic motivation is understandably the more desirable. Young people who are intrinsically motivated are curious about life, eager to be involved in activities and quick to participate, to 'have a go'. In short, they are flourishing. We find ourselves embracing their self-direction and community spirit. Their energy is a pleasure to behold. Intrinsic motivation is the foundation of positive connections, positive behaviour and positive learning.

As parents, life feels a lot more pleasant when our kids are intrinsically motivated by the things we would like them to do. We enjoy not having to waste our energy on continual attempts to persuade them to engage with learning, socialising … living.

But when our ten-year-old doesn't want to go to school, our twelve-year-old doesn't want to join afterschool activities, and our teenager doesn't seem to want to do much at all, we easily become frustrated, and worry that our children are not engaging in the things they need to pursue for academic and career success. More importantly, we worry that they will grow up without self-determination, unable to pursue goals for themselves or lead a meaningful life. We may also feel pretty exhausted if we are trying to be intrinsically motivated for them.

The Problem with Prizes

It can very tempting to resort to bribery to try to get our kids to act or engage with a task. We may set up a sticker chart to encourage them to complete household chores, or offer dessert for eating vegetables, or a new phone for achieving high grades in tests and exams.

In a world built on the shoulders of marketing giants, we have developed mainly extrinsically driven approaches to bringing up kids. But, intrinsic motivation cannot be increased with extrinsic temptations.[2,3,4,5] Still, it seems that from the moment they can walk, toddlers are given smiley faced stickers simply for 'turning up' at kindy gym. From early childhood to old age, we are encouraged to work harder, play harder and spend more money so that we may 'reap the rewards' of our success.

As adults, the lure of prizes dominates our daily lives in many and varied forms. Corporate high flyers push through exhaustion and high blood pressure with thoughts of large Christmas bonuses. Tired parents return to a café to claim their seventh coffee for free. We are encouraged to play games with electronic medals, count our steps for the prize of reaching a 'milestone' and use social media to increase our likes and follows. Businesses the world over know that people will work towards rewards and awards, whether tangible, electronic or emotional, at least in the short term. Rewards, by their very definition, are tempting. We want that bonus, that prize, that recognition. It's a promise of a happier life, and so we comply.

The focus on extrinsic rewards is most pronounced in the world of advertising. Every flashing Facebook ad tells us that our lives would be better, brighter and bigger, if only we had that new 'thing' in our lives. Billboards everywhere offer the rewards of better health, better looks, greater popularity or a sense of success, if we only do 'this' or buy 'that'. Marketers do not want us to find contentment in the moment, they want us to discontentedly work towards a better outcome … and then another even better outcome … and then one more …

The ancient Greek philosopher Epicurus suggested that the discontent created by advertising was our greatest cause of suffering and distress. How much more powerful is advertising in our modern technological world, where we see more than a thousand adverts every day telling us that we will be happier or more successful if only we buy 'this', or pay for 'that'? Adverts aim to persuade us to think of wellbeing as an outcome that arises from a purchase, rather than a product of living well. I don't think it is a simple coincidence that as the power and reach of advertising offering its extrinsic rewards increases, happiness and wellbeing diminish.

One of the scariest aspects of reward-driven living is the way in which we, as parents and educators, attempt to motivate and control our kids with carrots on sticks. We may say 'carpe diem' to our kids, but we encourage them to live for the reward they will receive later.

'Tidy your room and you can watch TV.'

'Do well at school and you'll get a good job.'

Some children are even rewarded for receiving rewards. Your child proudly brings home a merit certificate and what do you do? Place it triumphantly on the fridge and heap mountains of praise on the glowing winner.

In reality, the only person we can effectively motivate, in our homes or in our classrooms, is ourselves. Bribery may garner short-term compliance, but it leads to a loss of intrinsic motivation, an unhealthy outcome focus, and feelings of resentment as we rely on other's judgement of our actions.

Many of our schools can be the worst culprits, even while extolling the benefits of 'engaging in the process of learning'. Teachers want 'to motivate' whole classes of children; they want compliance and to keep everyone under control. Students around the developed world are persuaded to behave with offers of gel pens, class parties and other forms of payment. Young students are enticed with gleaming stationery for simply 'being nice' to one another or managing to sit still. Older children work for merit certificates, lucky dip prizes and class movies. Some schools even embrace the token economies of 1970s psychiatric hospitals, giving children tokens for desirable behaviour.

While it is true that most teachers understand the importance of developing positive relationships with their students, these precious relationships are all too frequently undermined by entrenched reward systems that dictate a power imbalance between teacher and student. The teacher becomes the judge and the student the compliant but ultimately resentful subject.

Similarly, many teachers embrace the value of creating a cohesive classroom community but find their strategies to actually build cohesion and community are compromised by a context that favours rewards and competition among the students. Worst of all is the well-meaning attempt of teachers to build cohesion by getting their class to work 'together' towards a class reward. Here, children are pitted against each other in terms of their contribution – winners may lead their peers to victory, but losers are responsible for a fail. Instead of the cohesive, motivated class of their good intentions, teachers end up with mini-gladiators fighting for recognition and survival.

'But wait!' I hear you cry, 'surely rewards must have benefits for kids or they would not be used so widely. Even wellbeing programs use rewards – they would not use the promise of prizes if this strategy didn't work … would they?'

Well, yes and no.

Certainly, the promise of extrinsic rewards often appears to get results, notably in the short term. Consider the room full of children who complete their projects when given the possibility of a class party. Or the teenager who works harder than ever in hope of getting an expensive new gadget.

The thing is – and this is a very important thing – rewards encourage students to focus on getting the reward, the desired outcome. The reward system works by increasing extrinsic motivation. But, because they ensure that kids' attentions are diverted from process to prize, they act to diminish intrinsic motivation and engagement in the learning (or behaviour) that the kids are being rewarded for.

Our reward-driven way of life sprang out of the behaviourism of the 1970s and 1980s, which itself was built on the behavioural conditioning discoveries of Ivan Pavlov. In the 1890s, Pavlov showed us that dogs will salivate at the sound of a bell if the bell has been consistently paired with food being offered. The dogs learned to behave (come when called) due to the offer of an extrinsic reward (dinner!). This understanding of animal training was translated into the 'training' of prisoners and psychiatric patients in the 1970s, where the controlling techniques frequently led to short-term compliance. But they also led to long-term resentment, loss of autonomy and independence, and increased institutionalisation. Many prisons and hospitals are now doing things very differently. It would be great if schools could also change ...

Children are not pets who we want to be obedient and compliant, under our control for life. As much as we love them, most of us hope our children will one day leave home and make independent, positive choices that do not require our approval. As such, training our children to live under our control, or worse still under the control of others, is never a good plan.

We hope that our children will choose a career, a relationship, a life that is intrinsically motivating. A life that engages them and provides them with meaning and purpose. We want our children to believe they have had a chance to live their life, their way. We certainly don't want them to lead a life based on impression management and the need to be rewarded with approval. We don't want them to work hard at school in order to get a good job, to get a big house, to get a promotion, to retire with a gold watch and then to finally wonder when their life will begin.

There are many adults who have no idea what they want to do with their life. Perhaps you are one of them. These are people who have learned to focus on outcomes and the desires of others, rather than on finding their own passion and intrinsic rewards.

Motivational expert and author Alfie Kohn describes a study in which two matched groups of children were invited to play with some wooden puzzles.[6] The members of one group were offered a reward for their time, the others were not. After each group had played with the puzzles they were left alone, to wait for their parents. During this waiting time they were filmed. The ten children who had been rewarded for their participation showed no interest in playing with the puzzles (which were still in the room) during this waiting time. In contrast, eight of the ten children who had not been paid continued to play with the puzzles while waiting.

Kohn discusses the long-term problems of extrinsic motivation in his book *Punished by Rewards*. He cites a study which found that children who are given a reward for reading in grade three are less likely to read for pleasure in grade six than children who were not given rewards when younger. Considering the profusion of extrinsic reward systems on offer for early learners, this is a major concern.

A student may read more books because they are receiving tokens or pizza, but they will generally pay less attention to the content of those books. They are also more likely to choose books that they can quickly finish, rather than books that interest or engage them. And if you don't read books you engage with when you are young, you are less likely to read at all when you are older.

The temptation of rewards distracts children from focusing on the process of learning academically, socially and emotionally; they are cut off from the many intrinsic rewards that come with this. Without intrinsic motivation, we lose engagement, interest and the possibility of connecting with our lives. And connecting with our lives is the essence of living well. Extrinsic rewards may lead to short-term compliance in the classroom (or the boardroom), but the costs are high.

Epicurus observed that a continual focus on outcome fosters an ongoing discontentment and dissatisfaction with where we are at, here and now. If we need to continually work to gain something better, then this means that life can't be quite right now. Imagine shopping and seeing something you would really love to have but can't afford. Suddenly it becomes so very hard to live without it – and this is all the more so if you are a child.

Of course, sometimes in life we need to do things that we are not totally enamoured with, in order to get something we want. And it is not wrong to want to experience the satisfaction that comes from achieving a goal. The problem is when it becomes a continual focus on outcomes that are removed from the nature of the task at hand, especially outcomes that take the form of extrinsic rewards. Education should be structured around the love of life-long learning, not the achievement of awards, rewards and grades.

In *Punished by Rewards* Alfie Kohn describes many other studies that support his conclusions. In one study, children were divided randomly into two groups to taste test a yogurt drink. In one group the kids are paid for their time and in the other group they are not. Both groups rated the drink as pleasant when taking part in the taste test. However, one week later, the kids who were paid were significantly less interested in having more of the drink than were the kids who had taste tested the drink for free. Simply by being paid (rewarded) to take part in the taste test, the kids were less engaged in the test itself, and consequently less interested in the drink one week later. By focusing on the outcome (the extrinsic reward) they engaged less with the process of enjoying the drink.

This study, like many hundreds of other studies, shows us that the only motivation developed by handing out rewards, is that of gaining those rewards.

Fabulous … Amazing … Good Job …

So, what about praise? If it is such a bad idea to reward kids for learning or behaving well, is it also a bad idea to say: 'Good job!'? According to world-leading expert in motivation Edward Deci, the answer to that depends on our intentions. If you offer extravagant praise for someone's behaviour to encourage them to repeat that behaviour in the future, then your intention is to garner compliance. In which case beware!

But if you are offering genuine praise of someone's personal development as a self-determined individual, then this is great. However, the praise you offer must genuinely support that person's intrinsic motivation; it should not simply reflect your judgement of their performance.

Consider Jack practising playing the piano. If you genuinely love his playing, then tell him. This is sharing your authentic pleasure at his performance. But if you praise Jack with, 'Good job, great playing,' merely as a sign of your approval of his practice, you are using praise as a reward to garner control over him.

As social beings we might enjoy the praise – after all, we want to feel we belong and are appreciated – but we do not want to be controlled. It is far better to ask Jack how he feels about mastering such a tricky piece or what he liked best about the music he is learning – such questions help him to see the intrinsic benefits of what he is doing. Support the opportunity for his practice by providing time and space for him to do this but don't judge his playing. Let Jack learn to love to play without needing your approval.

Extrinsic rewards not only diminish essential intrinsic motivation, they impair the quality of performance, impact badly on our relationships, and lead to long-term dissatisfaction with learning, whether it is of an academic, a social or an emotional nature.

When kids are rewarded for their behaviour in schools, they may initially show more compliance, but they end up with a less positive attitude to the teacher and to the other students in a classroom. Classes that are run on the basis of reward systems end up as more disruptive and less desirable places to be by the end of the year, compared to those that focus on the processes of building cohesion and shared values.

Don't underestimate children. They may be younger than adults, and easily bamboozled with our words, but they read faces far better than we can. They know when we 'mean it' and when we don't. They can see when you mean the praise and when you are simply aiming for control. Little Sophie may be excited to receive that gel pen for paying attention in class. But, she knows that her prize is wrapped in approval not love.

Extrinsic reward systems are so entrenched in every aspect of our western lives that it may seem inconceivable not to use them. But if we continue to focus on outcomes and rewards, we will continue to hijack our attempts to elevate wellbeing with mindfulness, classroom cohesion or engagement in the process of learning.

As both parent and educator, I appreciate that despite sound research support, the idea of letting go of rewards and an outcome focus can sound decidedly scary. In particular, the loss of a reward system can leave a very large hole in any behaviour management plan.

The solution lies in the understanding and development of healthy cohesion.

If we can develop healthy cohesion in our schools – where individuals feel they belong and feel connected to others – we will have built the basis for better levels of wellbeing, resiliency, unity and positive behaviours in families. Improved cohesion in schools is also significantly related to better mental health, greater intrinsic motivation, greater participation, more pro-social behaviour, greater success in terms of academic, social and emotional outcomes and ultimately a safer, more equitable education system.

The development of cohesion – at the class and at the whole school level – is the subject of the next chapter.

CHAPTER SEVEN

Building Cohesion

*To ensure that effective policies and practice
are internalised into each member of a school
community, schools need to develop cohesion
and an environment where desirable values
are the norm. We do things because they are
'the norm', not because someone tells us that
doing something is a great idea.*

COHESION IS THE POWERFUL social glue that turns us from human beings into people.[1,2] It is the glue that binds us to every element of our social context. When there is strong healthy cohesion in class-rooms and school communities, staff and students feel connected to those around them; they're on the same page with them. They feel they belong, that they are part of the team, with shared values and a shared sense of what is normal.

In the language of social psychology, social cohesion develops out of 'personal attraction' between members of any given group and the sharing of rules and norms within that group. 'Personal attraction' is a term used to represent a liking for others based on shared traits and goals, and a sense of belonging to the group as a whole. Once personal attraction has bound members of a group together, the members of the group will internalise shared values and goals as the conditions for group membership.

From 'Human Being' to 'Being a Person'

In Chapter One, I discussed wellbeing as a social phenomenon, as a healthy interaction with a healthy context. Not only is wellbeing governed by our interaction with our context, so too are our beliefs, values, thoughts and behaviours. In fact, just about every aspect of our identity is influenced and shaped by the social world around us, and our interaction with that world.

Let's think about fashion. If flared jeans were to come back into fashion (and I secretly wish they would), most teens would initially look at them as relics of the past, unattractive and undesirable. Yet, over time, they would be influenced by increasingly persuasive images of 'cool' people wearing flares in marketing campaigns and popular culture. They would see flares on young models in adverts, on mannequins in teenage clothes shops, on YouTube and on TV stars and eventually on their peers in the street.

Before they could utter the words 'bell bottom' they would be buying a pair of flares of their own, and very likely believing they had made an independent, individual choice in doing so. But according to social psychology, they would have internalised a normative attitude (wanting a particular style of jeans) which had stemmed from the group to which they want to belong (the group of 'cool and popular adolescents').

Meanwhile you, as an adult, may be less inclined to see flares as attractive, simply because you are not interested in being a part of adolescent culture – unless you are like me, and get caught in the nostalgia of the flared fashion of your youth.

It is true that not all adolescents would succumb to the trend. Those who felt they were on the outside of mainstream adolescent culture would be less likely to internalise a new adolescent cultural norm. We do not internalise the beliefs of a group unless we feel we belong.

In classrooms and indeed in whole school communities, students who are attracted to a particular social group internalise the norms of that group. The more attached they are to the group members, the more they incorporate the group norms into their own social identity.

This is why it is imperative that we take time to build cohesion in our classrooms and schools, and that we promote desirable norms within these social settings. We want to create ways to ensure that students feel a sense of attraction to the classroom group as a whole, and to the wider school community. We also want to ensure that class membership is conditional upon healthy social norms.

Helping young people to form into a cohesive class group can seem extremely time consuming and effortful for any busy teacher, an extra investment of energy for long-term pay-offs, not short-term gain. But trying to educate a fractured, non-cohesive class takes far more effort in the long term, so I think it is imperative the attempt be made. As educators we need to focus on 'the long game' for our students' wellbeing and engagement in learning.

The Development of Social Cohesion in Classrooms and School Communities

In the absence of any active strategies of cohesion, students will naturally form into social groups of between five and seven people,[3,4,5] based on shared goals and ideals. This means that within any classroom, there could be five or six distinct groups. For instance, one group could be united by a shared desire to achieve high grades whereas another could reflect a desire to avoid academic learning altogether. Groups could be united by the love of sport or socialising, or on the basis of drinking, drug use or wanting to be thin.

Some of these groups may appear to support healthy norms and behaviours whereas others most definitely would not. Either way, the existence of several small groups can hinder the class from becoming a united whole. Competition and distrust may arise between conflicting groups. Group members often unite in a shared dislike of outsiders. They may also join forces in dislike of an in-group member who fails to adhere to the conditions of group membership. Thus, kids in a group bound together by academic excellence may openly disapprove of a group bound by a disdain for academic skills, and they may reject a member who fails an exam, letting down the 'standard required'. A group of sports enthusiasts may look down on those who follow more sedentary pursuits, and may withdraw their support from a member who is no longer able to 'make the team'.

It is easy to see that a fragile basis for group membership can lead to fragile relationships for many students. Vulnerable students who are struggling to meet conditions for group membership have to contend with a constant fear of rejection. A sense of belonging is vital for student wellbeing,[6] but the group to which each student belongs needs to be bound by healthy, flexible conditions for membership.

Even when class norms are healthy and well established, teachers need to pay attention to ensuring that all students feel they belong to the class. In most classrooms there will be students who are not paying attention, not listening and not engaging, although these are the norms the rest of the class are observing. These kids have not internalised the classroom norms because they do not have sufficient connections to others or a sense of belonging: they desperately need social guidance and support. Sadly, in many schools these are the children who are often pushed further out of the group, out of the classroom altogether, and sometimes even out of the school.

Rewards and punishments may bring a disruptive child to the river of compliance, but only cohesion will keep them drinking. Instead of paying disconnected kids to behave, or threatening them if they don't, we need to help them connect to a world where positive behaviour is normal.

If you are a teacher who reaches the end of each day exhausted, stressed and burned out, I would guess that you have very little overall cohesion in your classes. Most likely, you have found yourself dealing with competing subgroups, who may or may not want to learn, and with 'outsiders' who do not feel they belong. You may have managed to establish yourself as the leader of a group of keen academic learners, but probably feel estranged from many of the other kids in the room.

Building a Cohesive Classroom

If a classroom can establish cohesion for all students and staff, with healthy conditions for membership, then great things can happen.

So how can we do this?

Foremost, teachers need to develop positive relationships with *all* of their students. Easily said, but a goal that takes energy, determination, skill and nerve to achieve. I say 'nerve' because teachers need to prioritise the process of building personal relationships and an overall class identity *before* they start laying down the rules and trying to teach the curriculum.[7,8,9] This means making the time to develop social cohesion at the start of each year, the start of each term, the start of each day, so that students feel valued as individuals, rather than simply as members of a class. The teacher's first skills must be to know how to listen, how to guide students socially and emotionally and how to help outsiders come in from the cold.

Putting positive relationships first is at the core of running a school on equitable and cohesive values and ideals rather than competition, inequity and hierarchies. *In cohesive communities it is normal to help others who are in need and treat people with respect.* Healthy norms are equitable, clear and well established, and are visible in every area of the learning environment.

Norms not Rules

Norms and rules are not the same thing. It does not matter what rules apply to the classroom, it is the established norms that guide the behaviour of those who feel they belong.[10,11] Rules are written down and made explicit whereas norms are established through the repetition of certain behaviours and reinforced with every element of social context. Norms are the true behavioural guides within any group.

For example, as a teacher, you may have made a classroom rule that students must be quiet when you speak. However, if you can't get the class to be quiet unless you start shouting, you may have inadvertently established a norm allowing the class to be noisy until you raise your voice.

Your school may state that every student is equally valuable, yet if it operates within a context of competition and hierarchical learning, the norm of inequity will prevail. Mission statements, though well-intentioned, rarely have impact if the school context is not addressed.

The only truly effective way for school rules to become classroom norms is to ensure that rules are reflected in the school social context,[12] and that every child feels a sense of belonging to their classes and wider school community. Once a child experiences this 'personal attraction' in their school community, they internalise the social norms of that community and act accordingly.

Getting to Know You

When faced with a new class, teachers can start the process of developing cohesion by learning their students' names as quickly as possible. This may mean asking students to wear name badges for the first week or put name cards on their desks. When someone uses our name, it creates a positive feeling in us and provides a simple yet powerful connection between us. We know the conversation is personal to us; directed at us.

Positive student–teacher relationships are developed when a teacher takes time to get to know a student as a whole person, beyond their role as a student. The process begins with simple but powerful steps such as asking students how they are doing, how their weekend was; taking an interest in their hobbies, their family and their overall wellbeing. It comes from developing a genuine, caring, non-judgemental relationship with that person.

Some kids may not find consistently healthy values or a sense of belonging at home, but they can still thrive as a member of a healthy school environment if they feel like they belong to that environment. This is another important reason school communities need to make cohesiveness a priority.[13]

Teachers can develop positive relationships with their students even when they don't especially relate to – or like – their behaviour or situation. For example, if a student is excited about a concert or a sporting team, a teacher can embrace that student's passion, even if they don't like that music or sport. If a student is anxious about a forthcoming test, or having a hard time at home, a teacher can empathise with difficult feelings even if they can't relate to the student's fear. We all know how it feels to be calm or anxious, happy or sad, even if it is in response to different things, to different degrees, expressed in different ways.

And of course, there will be students in every class who make the practice of empathy highly challenging. I doubt it is possible to like everyone, and not everyone is easily likable. However, it *is* possible for every teacher to find some common ground and empathy with just about every child, once they have the will to do so.

Teachers can deepen their relationship with students by simply introducing themselves as a person beyond their role as a teacher, with a full name, a family, a life outside of school. Such pieces of personal information help students to engage with teachers in the classroom. A teacher may fear losing authority with this kind of familiarity, but it is far better for ultimate classroom health to build shared goals with positive connections and empathy.

Teachers can also be instrumental in the development of overall class unity. Active intervention with non-competitive activities, games and humour all help build cohesion across the entire class and inhibits the development of conflicting subgroups. Spending the first five minutes of a 50-minute class playing a fun, non-competitive game helps everyone to feel part of the group. The brain breaks mentioned in Chapter Four work well to build cohesion as do opportunities for kids to share personal stories and listen to one another. Personal stories don't have to be deep and meaningful in nature or centred on feelings (though they can be). They can focus on humorous anecdotes or special moments. In this way 'getting to know you' takes on a more organic approach.

There are some excellent relationship-building programs with good research evidence to support them. As with any wellbeing program though, teachers have to be careful not to counteract their positive impact with unnecessary class competition and inequitable teaching the rest of the time. As soon as students are pitted against each other with tests, awards or ability grouping, cohesion and positive relationships suffer. It is the power of 'show over tell': explicit teaching of social and emotional competencies has to be backed up with real life contextual wellbeing.[14,15]

Another major strategy for cohesion building is to let students develop a sense of ownership over their class through choice and control. Choice and control are key ingredients of play, as we discussed in Chapter Four, and they also help children feel they are autonomous and can take charge of their learning. Primary school children benefit from being allowed to decorate their classroom along with the teacher, rather than have the teacher create the class for them. Students of all ages benefit when they have a say in the arrangement of desks, lighting, heating and what goes on the classroom walls. All students benefit when they have a say in the establishment of class rules, in the timetable (where possible), and even in the way in which learning takes place: in small groups or pairs, in projects or in a more linear fashion. The more that students are given real opportunities for autonomy and ownership over their everyday classroom life, the more engaged they will be in learning and with one another.

Making Wellbeing Normal

The normalisation of desired behaviours is supported when both students and staff set the rules. Teachers can begin this process by asking students to establish their own explicit class goals. Then the classroom rules become a necessary path to attaining these desired goals, rather than a restrictive end in themselves. This exercise equates to discussing the 'class goals and rules' with all students in the class.

The shared rules of class group membership could usefully include demonstrating 'mutual respect' and 'support' for others and taking a 'non-judgemental attitude' and 'compassionate approach' to building relationships. Such rules are more easily said than done. It would be good if teachers could steer the class towards coming up with these goals themselves. A rule has greater impact when you have chosen it yourself.

Once the class goals, rules and ideals have been discussed by the class, they need to be agreed upon by the whole class. Dan Ariely's work on honesty shows that students are far more likely to turn class rules into norms if they have agreed to them first.[16] The form of agreement may include all students signing a copy of the rules, which are then put on display.

Teacher and students then need to work together to ensure that class behaviour abides by the agreed rules. Norms develop through repeating desired behaviours, and contextual support, not through repeated verbal reminders.[17] The more a class follows the rules in their daily activities, the more likely the rules will become norms. It also follows that the more the rules are broken, the more 'not following the rules' will become the normal way to behave.

Assumptions of Honesty and Trust

Normative behaviour can also be encouraged with a contextual assumption of normality. The more we treat others according to the norms we would like them to follow, the more they will follow these norms. For example, people who are trusted are more likely to act in a trustworthy and honest way.

In 2013 in the district of Erode in India, the Isha Vidhya elementary school decided they needed a new way for students to purchase stationery items. The nearest stationery shop was too far away, and the school did not have sufficient funds to hire someone to sell stationery on the premises. As a solution, the school set up an 'honesty shop' stocked with priced stationery items and a bowl for money. Students are instructed to leave the correct change in the bowl and take the items they have purchased. There is no-one to monitor the students, no CCTV and no alarm.

After one week in operation, not only was it evident that no-one had stolen any stationery, the shop had actually made a profit. Students who had not had the exact change had left a little more, rather than not enough. The shop was thriving. What's more, the honesty shop has made a profound impact on other areas of school life. Feeling trusted and in control of their stationery purchasing, the children behave in a more honest and trustworthy way in all aspects of school life.

The success of the shop has been so profound that many other schools in the area have set up their own honesty shops, to encourage overall honesty and trust within the school community. A ninth grader sums up the impact of the honesty shop in her school:

After all the shop has been opened for us and how can one be dishonest? It has shaped our conscience and disciplined us to be honest even when no one is there to monitor us. No one really believed that such a system could work. We are really proud of our school.

Kavitha, ninth grade, letter to the *Deccan Herald*,
19 October 2013[18]

I would love to see schools all over the world set up their own honesty shops, whether for stationery, books, second-hand items or refreshments. Yet I am sure there are plenty of teachers and parents who would consider this a lovely ideal, but not viable: some students simply can't be trusted. Still, the bottom line is, no-one can be trusted unless we trust them first.

A few years ago, the music department of a large high school in Queensland decided to open the music staff room to their students. (It was believed that some students were struggling with their behaviour due to a lack of lunch and a safe space to hang out.) The staff made sandwich toasters, sliced bread and cheese available, and told the students they could make themselves toasties during breaks. This innovation (and very possibly the toasted sandwiches!) had a profound, positive impact on every member of the music department community. For example, staff reported less conflict and greater engagement in classroom learning. Students demonstrated more honest behaviour and took greater responsibility for their learning. What's more, despite the fact that staff often left phones, car keys and other personal possessions lying around on the staff room tables, nothing was ever stolen during the two years following the program's instigation.

There is so much we could do to create a norm of honesty and trust within our school environments. Besides honesty shops and open staff rooms we could simply unlock doors at lunch time and take padlocks off lockers. Yes, it is a risk to remove a lock and make your possessions vulnerable. But I believe it is more risky to encourage a culture of mistrust and poor behaviour.

Honesty and trust are two of the greatest virtues of a civilised society. Along with sincerity and integrity they promote freedom, community and safety. If we are honest with ourselves, we make healthier, happier choices in life. The man who is forever having one last cigarette or the woman who is continually joining that yoga class *next* week are both deceiving themselves, and potentially creating significant long-term problems.

In our relationships with others, honesty and trust enable us to create intimacy that is simply not possible in the face of deceit. Honesty comes with a sense of our authenticity and our own truth, both of which allow for a deeper, more genuine connection in our social encounters. When we are honest, we are presenting a true face, not some camouflaged version of ourselves built on pretence for impression management. Consider when you have felt the need to present a false smile at a social occasion: how exhausting it can be to forgo your own truth in favour of another's social rules.

In our broader communities, whether at home, school or work, honesty breeds a sense of trust which in turn leads to a greater feeling of belonging and of emotional and physical safety. We feel empowered and powerful in communities where we don't have to continually guard our possessions through fear of theft or guard our words for fear of 'saying the wrong thing.'

Honesty and trust are at the core of all our healthiest relationships, no matter what our differences may be. If young people feel a part of an honest school community then they are more likely to internalise honest and trusting behaviours.

In a healthy educational context, policies and practice support the development of healthy, honest relationships between members of all classes and school communities, and the development of a sense of belonging in all school groups. A healthy educational context promotes desired beliefs, attitudes and behaviours through the development of social norms. It shows young people how to behave, rather than tells them what to do.

Teachers are under continual pressure to make headway with a dauntingly large curriculum, so it is a big ask that they regularly find time for gluing the class together. But that time willingly spent on building cohesion will save an enormous amount of wasted time and energy throughout the rest of the year.

A happy class is a cohesive class is a productive class.

CHAPTER EIGHT

The Importance of Teacher Wellbeing

Even when programs to support youth wellbeing have been found to work in experimental conditions, they rarely stand a chance if delivered by stressed and overloaded teachers. Wellbeing is about 'show' far more than about 'tell'. Staff need to be socially and emotionally competent if they are to be models for social and emotional learning.

HEALTHY RELATIONSHIPS FORM THE foundation of a positive classroom and school environment; they also provide a solid foundation for academic and emotional learning to take place.

'You can have thirty computers in your classroom, but it doesn't matter unless you get the relationships right,' said a teacher participating in Helen Cahill's 2004 study on school relationships.[1] I can vouch for this, from my own experience. When I moved from the UK to Australia to live, I did so alone. One of the most challenging issues I faced was not being able to share my new experiences with family and friends – something Miles Franklin articulated very well: 'Someone to tell 'it' to is one of the fundamental needs of human beings.'

The productivity and enjoyment of our work can be made or destroyed by the quality of our working relationships. Similarly, our family connectedness is defined through our relationships with our family members. In fact, beyond our basic needs for survival, relationships – and the people we have relationships with – are all that really matter in life. You do not have to be a psychologist to recognise the value of positive relationships, and positive people, in every area of human existence.

Yet we so often fail to give positive relationship development the time and attention it needs and deserves in our schools. And we fail to give full support to the people responsible for developing positive relationships and cohesion across the school community – teachers, school leaders, parents and of course, the students themselves.

At the 2004 National Educators conference in Western Australia I presented a talk on the importance of creating a nurturing classroom environment. I subsequently expanded my talk into a chapter for the conference book *Checking the Pulse*.[2] This chapter was one of my first publications exploring the development of a healthy context in schools.

In the chapter, I discussed my research exploring children's subjective understandings of wellbeing at school. I found that children and pre-teens conceptualised a nurturing classroom environment as one in which they felt emotionally safe, developed intimacy with significant others and felt a sense of belonging to their immediate social community. I concluded: 'the fundamental basis for the creation of a nurturing environment is the development and maintenance of positive social relationships throughout a child's life.' This same research forms the core of this book, for it suggests that positive relationships lie at the heart of Contextual wellbeing.

Ten years later I led a similar project with my Positive Schools co-chair Neil Porter and our team member Fenny Muliadi.[3] The 2014 project explored 458 responses about school-related beliefs from 21 primary and secondary schools across Australia. As part of the project, we asked students to answer open questions about what they thought 'made a school a positive school' and what 'made a class fun to be in'.

More than 40 per cent of the students told us that positive school-based relationships were imperative in making a class fun to be in. Moreover, positive relationships were believed to be fundamental for defining all aspects of education in positive terms. The project found that although students associate schools with academic achievements, their relationships with their friends, teachers and other school staff members play the biggest part in determining the emotional quality of their schooling experience.

When children enjoy positive relationships at school, they generally perform better academically and in sports, and have greater self-esteem and self-worth.

Back in 2004, I had suggested that resiliency stems from the development of meaningful social relations, an idea supported by many acclaimed experts on resilience. Child psychologist and author Andrew Fuller talks extensively about the need to understand and support a 'resilience mindset' in young people with co-author John Hendry.[4] In 2005, Fuller suggested that we can improve the resilience of young people in three main ways, the first being to: 'Improve the quality of connections, friendship, compassion and forgiveness in schools, families and communities.'[5] The second and third ways are through social emotional learning and student empowerment.

Following up on these views on the importance of relationships, Fuller conducted research in 2014 with more than 16,000 young people, and concluded: 'We know that the most powerful antidote to suicide, violence and drug abuse is the sense of belonging people have in their lives.'[6]

Positive relationships build students' resiliency and mental health and enhance their capacity for learning.[7,8]

Teaching Students Relationship Skills

It is vital that we pay attention to the way in which young people create relationships, and to the values, attitudes and social skills of the people they create relationships with. Healthy students nurture healthy relationships. And healthy relationships nurture healthy students.

An increasing number of programs and initiatives across Australia, and indeed the rest of the world, explicitly support the development and maintenance of positive relationships among students. These programs cover a long list of topics including: communication skills, assertiveness training, social emotional learning, difference, discrimination, inclusion, bullying prevention, pro-social behaviour and conflict resolution. Many initiatives also provide structured and unstructured opportunities for participants to practise their relationships skills and develop healthy relationships in formal and informal settings. Some of the best programs I have come across include Sue Roffey's Circles Solutions,[9] and Steve Heron's BUZ program.[10]

In our technological age, it is equally vital that young people are supported in the healthy development of online relationships, particularly on social media. Amongst the increasing amount of literature on young people and technology is *Real Wired Child*, an excellent book by adolescent psychologist Michael Carr-Gregg.[11] The book helps adults to understand and better support young people's online social world.

Experience and research both tell us that teaching students specific relationship strategies and skills can be a valuable use of school time. However, as with all individualised approaches to wellbeing, the strategies and skills that are taught to individuals must be reflected within the entire school context.

In the preceding chapters I have explored the development of contextual wellbeing with a focus on equity, cohesion and creativity. The ongoing development of cohesion within an equitable environment, along with opportunities for learning through collaboration and play, underlie the development of positive relationships and an overall sense of belonging within the school community.

The Importance of Teachers

A shiny, well-resourced school will not thrive without good educators. In contrast, good educators will always help students to thrive and can compensate for most of the problems of a run-down school. Thus, it is just as important to nurture social emotional competency, positive relationships and wellbeing among teachers, school leaders, support staff and parents. In particular, the support of teacher and school leader wellbeing needs to be made an absolute priority in every school.

Social emotional skills are modelled far more powerfully than they can ever be taught, a fact which is borne out in several studies by education experts. Among many others, Sue Roffey, Rebecca Collie and Jantine Spilt report that when school staff experience a state of wellbeing, with manageable stress levels and social and emotional competency, they can more effectively support positive relationships and social emotional learning in their students.[12,13,14]

Unfortunately, although schools know the importance of 'being well to do well', school leaders and teachers are rarely given the support they need in western schools. In fact, teaching is often found to be one of the developed world's most stressful jobs.

Reporting on teacher stress in 2011, Chris Kyriacou claimed that understanding teachers' stress is critical for the stability and effectiveness of educational systems worldwide.[15] A 2013 survey of 1000 K–12 public school teachers in the US by Martkow, Macia and Lee found that 59% of teachers reported being under great stress, a dramatic increase from the 35% identified in 1985.[16] These findings are consistent with a 2014 UK Gallup poll in which 46% of primary and high school teachers reported high daily stress during the school year. This is one of the highest reported stress levels among all occupational groups.[17]

According to M.T. Greenberg in a 2016 issue statement, 'Teacher stress and the resulting attrition are serious problems that negatively impact the quality of education, taking an emotional and psychological toll on school personnel and impacting student behaviour and achievement.'[18]

Teacher stress not only impacts badly on teachers, it has adverse effects on the young people in their care. In 2011, researchers Melissa Milkie and Catharine Warner found when teachers experienced high levels of stress, the children in their classes had higher rates of both internalising disorders (e.g. anxiety and depression, where the children 'internalised' their problems and kept them to themselves) and externalising disorders (e.g. disruptive behaviours and conduct disorders, where problem behaviours are externalised and have a significant impact on others).[19] Similarly, in 2016 in Canada, researchers Eva Oberle and Kimberley Schonert-Reichl found that teachers' self-reported burnout was linked to their students' physiological stress response.[20]

Students are often held individually responsible for dropping out of school, but researchers Gavin Duffy and Jannette Elwood found in 2013 that the majority of students who drop out of school reported negative relationships with their teachers or believed they had been disregarded by them.[21] In contrast, Ming-Te Wang and Stephen Peck reported in 2013 that positive teacher–student relationships protected adolescents against depression and misconduct throughout high school.[22]

Although many schools will devote occasional professional development hours to supporting teacher wellbeing and stress management, these are often seen as luxuries or add-ons to the 'real business' of teacher education.

It is time we gave teacher wellbeing and stress management the priority it deserves. This means ensuring that teachers are given wellbeing skills training and improved conditions for contextual wellbeing – starting with a manageable workload, good channels of communication, autonomy, status and respect, as well as opportunities to build positive relationships.

In Chapter Two I described the unmitigated failure of the DARE program. Another popular program which initially failed, although arguably less overwhelmingly, is the SEAL (Social and Emotional Aspects of Learning) program in UK high schools. The SEAL program aims to support children aged 3 to 16 years to develop the personal and social skills of self-awareness, managing their feelings, motivation and empathy. The program was rolled out in the early 2000s with great enthusiasm but little support for its actual delivery. In 2010, a damning review of the program was published by researchers who studied its impact in 22 schools.[23] The review concluded that the program was a failure, and that one of the biggest reasons for this was a lack of teacher skill and willingness to deliver the program well. More recent appraisals of the program have shown far more encouraging results, presumably as a result of greater investment in teacher training and support.

If we are to invest time, energy and money in introducing wellbeing programs into schools, we need to be very sure that the teachers delivering those programs have both the will and the skill to do so.

Immediate Strategies for Managing Teacher Stress

Ideally, teachers would not have to learn to deal with constant stress, or life overload, because they would be teaching in a healthy context that ensured they were thriving, rather than barely surviving – but achieving contextual wellbeing is a long-term project.

One of the key signs of life overload is a feeling of never having enough time. However hard we try, we never feel on top of things. Moreover, we often have an underlying fear that life will be over all too soon, before we ever get around to living it. In 2011 I wrote a book called *Life Overload* about stress and how to manage stress more effectively,[24] including some key strategies for dealing with life overload that can benefit staff and students within the school community.

1. **Learn to breathe**

   Stress is a physiological response to a perceived threat. Although work overload may come in a psychological package, we can still calm ourselves with physical intervention. When you experience a surge of stress related emotion, try taking ten seconds to take three deep breaths while deliberately dropping your shoulders back and down.

   Calmness comes one breath at a time.

2. **Develop your ideal self**

   Develop an identity in line with your ideal self rather than one that reflects the stress of today. The smallest of things can help. If you imagine being dressed a certain way in your ideal life, make a move to dress that way now. If you imagine having a certain hobby when you finish your exams, retire, or leave school, start that hobby on a smaller scale today.

   Take the time to create the life you want, albeit in small steps.

3. **Pay attention**

   Slow down from constant rushing and bring yourself back into the present. Try practising mindfulness meditation for five minutes every morning. Simply sit comfortably and breathe slowly. Count each breath from one to ten, and then start again. As you count, pay attention to your inner world (your thoughts coming and going, your mood, how your body feels) and your outer world (noises in the background, the temperature of the air).

   As you travel through life, grasp every opportunity to take time out from your check list and notice your day, right here and right now, for just a few precious minutes.

4. **Find some extraordinary time**

   No matter how busy you are, make a leap of faith and take two hours out of every week to do something that you really want to do. Something that is totally absorbing, creative and enjoyable. It could be starting piano lessons or simply catching up with good friends.

   Two hours of well spent extraordinary time will give you far more time for everything else.

5. **Simplify to survive**

   When life is overwhelming it is time to let go of some of the household chores or spending time with people who drain you rather than energise you.

   Make sure that the free time you have is spent doing the things you really want to do, not full of 'shoulds', 'oughts' and 'musts'.

6. **Do one thing at a time**

   Use timetabling to help reduce multi-tasking and frustration. Set goals by time not by outcome to help combat perfectionism. Remember, nobody can do more than one thing at a time with 100% of their attention; multi-tasking demands that you give less than 100% to multiple jobs.

   Real progress occurs one step at a time, one activity at a time.

7. **Be kind to yourself**

   Accept that life can be busy and challenging and that you don't have to be perfect. You can certainly aim to do your best, but you are not going to get everything right, every time. It really is all right to sometimes fail or to need to take several attempts to succeed.

   It is also crucial that you take time to nurture yourself. Make the time to look after yourself emotionally and physically so that you have the capacity to lead your busy life. Go out and get your hair done, get that massage, have a long bath. Eat good food, get enough sleep and make time for exercise. Even small acts of self-compassion and self-care can make a big difference to how you feel about everything.

The adventurer and author Tim Cope summed up his philosophy for dealing with life overload in one beautiful sentence, something he learned when trekking across Mongolia: 'If you have to rush in life ... then rush slowly.'

Parents as Partners

In a thriving school community *everyone* should feel included and valued. For this to come about, time and attention need to be given to supporting both individual and contextual wellbeing across various groups of people. A positive school nurtures the academic support staff, allied health professionals and other experts who contribute to school life, and, just as vitally, the parent body too.

Too often, conflicting goals, a fear of clashing agendas and a lack of ready communication result in parents being perceived as a separate group of stakeholders to teaching staff. They are seen as supporters of the school community, but not as fellow educators. But education is *not* something that happens only in the school grounds. Parents play a significant role in the education of their children, socially, emotionally and academically, and it is in the school's interests to recognise this.

Parenting expert Cathy Quinn considers it essential that schools and families recognise and respect that they each want the best for the children in their care. In her 2017 *Positive Times* article,[25] Cathy suggests that schools take a more strengths-based approach to forging positive partnerships with parents, identifying and recognising the equal but different strengths that parents and teachers bring to the education of their children. Teachers make a difference in the school environment; parents make a difference at home. Most parents have experience and knowledge about their child that comes from a deep, long-term emotional investment; teachers bring expert knowledge and experience about academic, social and emotional learning to the mix.

During my time as the chair of the Positive Schools conferences, I've heard many jokes at the expense of parents. Parents are called out for their 'helicopter' or 'lawn mower' strategies, meaning they are perceived as being overly involved with, and overly protective of their children. They may be labelled as demanding, or non-assertive or risk averse. I have heard parents accused of jeopardising their children's resiliency due to their unwillingness to let them take risks or fail. Other parents may be accused of putting their children in harm's way, paying too little time and attention to their online world.

Whatever the truth behind any of these charges, I am not sure that much of this criticism is helpful. Parents so often take their lead from their children's teachers. Many are keen to benefit from clearer guidelines about how best to handle creativity, risk and resilience in their children's development. It is inequity and the focus on competitive outcome embraced by so many schools, that makes it difficult for guidance to be meaningful.

It is hard for parents to support creativity when they see the time and attention paid to art, music, poetry and drama diminished in schools. It is confusing for them to appreciate the value of play and family time when their children come home with mountains of homework and instructions to 'work harder'. It is hard for them to tell their children to turn off their phones if the school lets them have their phones on all day. And it is hard not to encourage children to be competitive with each other when 'winning' seems to matter so much at every school assembly.

As much as educators are caught in a school system that needs reform, so too are parents. It is only through a desire for school educators and parents to work collaboratively that contextual wellbeing can become a truly sustainable and realistic means of helping young people to flourish ... at school, at home, in life.

CHAPTER NINE

The Spaces Around Us

We need to pay attention to the space around us at school. Consider the desks, observe what is on the walls, open the doors to ensure the corridors and public spaces belong to everyone. The physical space influences the behaviour and ultimate wellbeing of every member of the school community.

IN A 2014 ARTICLE in *Edutopia*, journalist and teacher Mark Phillips described his surprise when the tried and tested team building suggestions he made to a teaching colleague had fallen flat.[1] Everything became clear when Mark visited his colleague's classroom, which was housed in a dark and foreboding basement. He suggested that the teacher and students together invest time in creating a more positive environment, one that reflected the positive and engaged class they were in search of.

They took his suggestions on board wholeheartedly, and redecorated the room with colourful paint donated by parents and with lots of 'homely' touches. During the process of this transformation, the teacher reported a significant increase in cohesiveness and supportive social behaviours among the students. These changes continued in a positive direction after the students took residency in their newly decorated room.

Mark Phillips' story illustrates how important it is to pay attention to the physical context, whether for social or academic learning. It also serves as a reminder of how effective it is to involve the students in the process of creating their own positive environment, allowing them the opportunity to embrace their shared social identity within the classroom setting.

Reflections of Ourselves

Buildings exist as reflections of the attitudes, values and behaviours of their designers, owners and occupants. Whether in urban, rural or remote settings, people find themselves surrounded by reminders of their social identity. Even in the most rural location the land has often been transformed with farms, mines and settlements or marked by roads. Even the natural environment that we choose to leave untouched is symbolic of our cultural values.

Our physical environments shape us, just as they are shaped by us. The mythologist and author Joseph Campbell suggested that the height of the buildings in any town or city sends inhabitants a clear message about the hierarchy of governance.[2] Where church and cathedral spires once stood out among the rooftops, now it is often banks or other corporations which dominate the skyline. Advertising and marketing companies vie for prime position to influence our preferences and purchases.

The evidence of physical influence on our physical, social and psychological health is even more compelling within our homes and work spaces. Researchers have long reported the impact wrought by every aspect of the environment, from lighting, temperature, furnishings and colour to the messages we choose to write on our walls.[3]

Turning Back Time

One of the most fascinating experiments exploring the impact of our physical context is Ellen Langer's 1979 'counter clockwise experiment'.[4] Langer conducted this experiment to explore the impact of social context on biological age. Eight men aged in their late seventies were invited to stay in a '1950s' holiday home for a week. The home, a converted monastery in New Hampshire, US, had been meticulously decorated with a 1950s theme. Everything in the building was representative of 1959, including the newspapers, the furnishings, the pictures on the walls and the activities on offer.

The eight men were invited to step back twenty years in time for a week, and to act as if it were indeed 1959. For example, they were asked to talk about 1950s news events in the present tense; invited to watch a movie from 1959 'as if it were a new release' and to listen to a 1950s sports match on the radio as if it were happening in real time.

In addition, the subjects were treated by staff as if they were men in their fifties, not their seventies, and not requiring any special care or attention. They were told not to bring current photos and not to refer to their 1970s lives in any way.

Before the experiment commenced, the men were assessed on a range of physical and psychological measures that are known to relate significantly with biological age. They were reassessed on the same measures once the experiment was completed.

The results were astounding. All participants had significantly improved on a variety of measures of their biological age over the course of the week. Their memory and overall cognitive abilities had improved; they were stronger, more agile and had improved appetites. Some even demonstrated better eyesight. It appeared that the changes in their context, largely their physical context, had impacted on every aspect of their physical functioning. Many of the men had been walking unsteadily at the start of the experiment, but they all joined in a spontaneous game of touch football while waiting for the bus to collect them at the end of the week.

Ground-breaking though it was, Langer's 'counter clockwise' study should be viewed with caution. It was based on only a small sample size and I have found no evidence of a longer-term follow-up with the men or of the study being replicated. Even so, the experiment gives us a significant example of the power of social context, including our physical surroundings, over every aspect of our health and wellbeing.

Despite the academic and media attention given to Langer's study, and other significant work looking at the impact of the physical environment, there remains a scarcity of research into the impact of the *school* physical environment. Nevertheless, we know that the school environment impacts on all areas of academic, social and emotional learning; we just have a long way to go in terms of understanding how to create a 'best possible' physical environment for any particular school.

We do know that the impact of the physical environment appears to be significantly affected by the behaviour of those using that environment. For example, the popularity of open plan classrooms in the 1980s could not make up for the lack of teacher commitment to open plan learning.[5] Many teachers ended up 'surviving' their open plan environments rather than using them well, and the potential benefits of teaching in flexible and collaborative learning spaces were often overshadowed by high noise levels and insufficient cooperation between staff and students.

If we are to change and develop the physical environment in a positive way, all those using the environment should understand its purpose and potential. Schools contemplating new designs should therefore stay clear of architectural determinism, in which it is the architect's vision that is realised rather than the vision of those using the space.

Owning Your Space

In the classroom transformation Mark Phillips wrote about in 2014, the benefits of any physical space are significantly increased if that space has been created by all those using it. An unattractive, messy classroom that every student has helped to create is a better learning environment than a beautiful room set up by only the teacher.

Contextual Wellbeing is a philosophy based on the idea that our wellbeing is embedded in our social context as much as it lies within us as individuals; it maintains that our identity extends beyond our physical selves into the various contexts in which we live. When students and staff work together to create not only positive classrooms but a positive whole school physical space, everyone has the chance to develop ownership over their contextual wellbeing, and a sense of belonging to the school environment.

For the rest of this chapter I want to explore the impact of the physical environment – the grounds, the buildings, the classroom – on teaching, learning and student wellbeing.

The Power of Outside

According to his 2012 report for the National Trust in the UK,[6] naturalist Stephen Moss estimates that the outdoors area around a child's home – in which they are free to roam – has decreased by over 90% in England since the 1970s. Moreover, he states that Britain's children watch, on average, almost two-and-a-half hours of TV per day, every single day of the year. In addition, they spend more than 20 hours a week online, mostly on social networking sites. As the children grow older their screen time expands still further. Britain's 11–15 year olds spend an average of seven and a half hours in front of a screen, every day.

The situation is similar in other developed countries. Yale University professor Stephen Kellert reported in 2015 that a typical child in the United States spent 90% of their time indoors,[7] often on screens. In fact, children as young as two were using a screen for an average of 30 hours a week, while school aged children averaged over 50 hours. These are alarming statistics, and I doubt they will improve in the immediate future. These same children devoted less than 30 minutes a day to free play outside in 2015, as opposed to their parents in the 1970s and 1980s, who spent four hours every day roaming outside.

I am not saying that technology is toxic or that screen-time is the single cause of this increasingly indoor life, but these findings do suggest that the rise of home-based technology plays a significant role in 'nature deprivation'. We need to find a better balance between onscreen and outside time in young people.

In his 2005 book *Last Child in the Woods*,[8] Richard Louv coined the term 'nature deficit disorder'. He argued that children growing up in today's world have a diminished ability to focus, to use their senses, to attend to their surroundings – in effect to be mindful – and are experiencing higher rates of physical and emotional illness

Stephen Moss's National Trust report[9] suggests that this disconnection with the outdoors and the natural environment is causing physical, emotional and intellectual deficits in children's learning and development. He believes outdoor play fosters all manner of cognitive, social and emotional learning through curiosity, observation, wonder, exploration, problem-solving and creativity.

Schools are well situated to help support 'outside time' and time in nature for young people, through the development of school grounds or with opportunities for visits to natural settings. Peter Pagels and colleagues in 2014 found that the set-up of the outdoor school environment significantly affected activity levels in Swedish students.[10] They suggest that outdoor design, as well as opportunities to use the outdoors, impact on physical activity levels on a daily basis. A child's attitude towards exercise has been found to lay the foundation for their habits as an adult and consequently for their ongoing quality of life and longevity.

Physical health and fitness are undeniably important, but the outdoor school environment offers far more in addition to these, as Stephen Kellert observed in 2015. 'In engaging with other life from redwood trees to hedgehogs, [children] encounter an endless source of curiosity, emotional attachment and a motivation for learning. In adapting to the ever-changing, often unpredictable natural world, they learn to cope and problem-solve.'

Kellert's work is supported by child psychologist Aric Sigman who, in 2007, found that exposure to nature significantly boosts concentration and self-control in children.[11] Sigman also identified significant improvements in children's mindfulness, reasoning and observational skills as well as on many academic measures including reading, writing and math.

These important findings have led to explicit instructions in the UK to embrace outdoor spaces for learning, especially in primary schools.[12,13,14] Scottish schools have become particularly known for their enthusiasm to reflect indoor learning in outside settings and with outside experiences.[15,16] They demonstrate how easily learning can take place outdoors, whether to enhance structured teaching or as an alternative to traditional in-class delivery.

Contextual wellbeing is most strongly supported when the school grounds provide opportunities for play in natural settings, beyond constructed playgrounds and the school oval. Spending time in nature, at any level of interaction, enhances our wellbeing, and great benefits occur when students have the opportunity to interact with the natural world around them as part of their educational journey.

A class mood can be lifted simply by taking the classroom outside to an undercover area or sheltered spot within sight of a natural setting. An art class can involve painting objects found outside or painting a landscape. Time spent gardening or building a structure from natural materials can draw on active learning in maths and science. Urban and nature visits can complement history and geography lessons, and just about any outdoor setting can provide inspiration for creative writing.

Just being outdoors can greatly benefit all students, and that includes excursions to museums, galleries and other places of interest that take them outside the school gates.

More than Bricks and Mortar

Physical characteristics of the school environment can impact on student health and wellbeing if they fall below a certain standard. In their 2005 literature review 'Produced for the Design Council', Steve Higgins and colleagues[17] identified solid evidence that poor lighting, high external noise and poor ventilation all appear to impact negatively on students and staff.

Many researchers conclude that lighting can cause a range of difficulties, including poor physical health and an inability to concentrate, and the majority hold that natural lighting is far superior to artificial. When artificial lighting is necessary, Karpen reported in 1993, full spectrum polarised artificial lighting is superior to lighting that creates glare and flicker when presenting at a convention.[18] However, not all researchers reported in the Higgins review believed that poor lighting had a detrimental impact on student health.

Poor air quality has a significant negative impact on student health, wellbeing and academic focus, as does excess heat or cold, Earthman found in 2004.[19] A high level of noise from outside a class has also been found to disrupt learning and diminish student focus.[20]

The type and position of classroom furniture also has an effect on student wellbeing. In 1999 Knight and Noyes[21] found that chair height and comfort can have an impact on student physical health as well as on their ability to focus in class and engage in class activities. Children and young people's physical shape and in particular, their height, varies enormously. It makes sense to embrace seating suitable for children of varied heights and physiques in any classroom set up.

The benefits of meeting basic standards for comfort are far reaching, and, interestingly, 'basic' appears to be all that is required. Higgins' 2005 'Impact of School Environments Review' suggests that once noise, seating, heat and light have all been brought to a comfortable level, there is no evidence for the value of creating a more 'luxurious' environment. Expensive, shiny new classrooms and school buildings may please stakeholders more than they add benefit to the school community.

When it comes to the colour of the walls, subdued, warm colours appear most beneficial in classrooms, especially for the wall containing the whiteboard. However, there is little united research favouring any particular set of colours. Rather, it seems that it is having *choice* over classroom wall colour that creates a positive impact on both staff and students.[22]

Overall, the available research brings us once again to the importance of feeling a sense of ownership over our immediate physical environment. It is the involvement of the school community that makes the most positive impact in the development of the physical context of the school. Once again, it is a reminder that schools need to be wary of architects' determinism or a school leader's unilateral visions when planning for change.

Our identity exists in the physical space around us and our sense of autonomy is connected to our sense of choice and control of that space. Many of us will have vivid memories of the décor of our teenage bedrooms. After all, a teenager's bedroom is generally a clear expression of their emerging identity. I remember feeling 'invaded' if my mother tidied my room for me, and enraged when my father suggested I remove my David Bowie posters in favour of something he regarded as more aesthetically pleasing. Our physical space matters, and having a sense of ownership over that physical space matters even more. It is the same when it comes to our schools: the most effective physical environments are created when the whole school community is consulted and involved in the process of change and development, from classroom décor to the shared spaces.

When it comes to high school, it is harder to promote student involvement in the decoration of classrooms than it is in primary school. Movement between rooms by both staff and students makes the process challenging, however, it does not make it impossible.

Students can still help with desk arrangements, creating displays in rooms they are taught in, and in daily decisions about acceptable noise, heating and lighting levels.

There is one aspect of the physical space that does benefit from complete teacher control, and that is the arrangements of desks and the class seating plan. Ideal desk arrangements vary according to different activities.[23] Desks in rows tend to support individual activities; a semi-circle aids class discussions and small clusters favour collaborative work. For this reason, easily movable chairs and desks are an ideal option in any primary or secondary class room.

Where students sit is significant. Research has shown that students placed in the front or centre of a classroom – sometimes referred to as the 'T zone' – tend to be perceived to be more likable and popular than their peers. Students seated at the outer edges are more likely to be seen as social outliers among their peers. Yvonne Van Den Berg and Antonius Cillessen reported research in 2015 showing that the impact of seating on judgements about student attractiveness is at its most pronounced at the start of the school year.[24]

Teachers therefore need to use care when considering who to seat where, and how frequently to move seating around, particularly at the beginning of term one. If students are given free rein to select seats, then popular kids may increase their popularity by placing themselves in the centre of the room whereas outliers stick to the edges. Overall, it makes sense to place anxious or shy students more centrally, to ensure they have a greater chance of establishing friendships and social support.

Voices from the Walls

When it comes to the school buildings and indoor physical spaces, consideration needs to be given to both the direct impact of the physical environment and the indirect messages conveyed within that environment. For the physical space acts as a powerful voice for the other domains of social context. In particular, it supports the creation and maintenance of the social norms and values of the classroom and the whole school community.

As a parent, staff member or student, consider what messages are being communicated to you as you walk through your school's physical space. What messages are being given out by the reception? The hallways? The canteen? The classrooms?

These covert messages say volumes about the true values of the school community, and they can have a far bigger impact on those values than overt policy or practice. A school reception displaying photos of community events and collective works of art is telling a very different story to the reception that displays sporting trophies and pictures of student leaders. These publicly placed visual messages are powerful influences on school culture and behaviour, and ultimately on student wellbeing.

Do the messages in the hallways and school hall inspire students and affirm that equity is important? Or do they suggest that education is a race you might win or lose?

Schools need to be cautious when creating public spaces to explicitly support positive values such as friendship, kindness and gratitude. It is good to draw attention to the importance of these elements of wellbeing, but it is important to be careful not to inadvertently end up drawing on unhealthy contexts such as control, compliance or quantifiable hierarchies during the process. For example, primary schools need to be sure that 'buddy benches' do not inadvertently suggest that the children who sit there are not good at making friends. Positive Education schools need to ensure that 'what went well' boards or 'gratitude walls' – set up to promote positive behaviours such as a focus on strengths and the development of gratitude – do not end up as negative judgements on those who cannot identify a recent positive experience. All schools need to reflect on whether a desire to promote positive behaviours such as kindness, gratitude or compassion, ends up as yet another competition among the students.

It is especially important that messages in the environment are framed in terms of positive outcomes rather than as stands against negative behaviours. For example, a sign that says 'friends look after each other' is stating a positive message about the pro-social behaviours desired in the school. In contrast, a message that states 'no bully zone' highlights that bullying is a problem that needs to be solved.

Whenever planning an initiative involving a public display within the school environment, it is vital that schools comprehensively 'unpack' that initiative *before* they present it for public view. They need to carefully examine the intentions (e.g. to convey information, build compliance or develop desired norms), the key words used (e.g. positive versus negative) and the powerful covert messages being delivered (e.g. that teachers' judgements of others matter or that student self-determination is vital).

Schools often attempt to support intrinsic motivation with extrinsic judgements of behaviour. In particular, there is a worrying trend for schools to reward students for simply being nice to each other, and then put these rewards on public display. This simply does not work. Extrinsic rewards may indeed garner short-term compliance but, as we saw in the chapter on motivation, giving a reward for positive social behaviour only ensures that empathy and compassion are diminished over time. All that will increase is a resentment of those acting as behavioural judges in the community.

Classroom décor is no exception to this rule. Cohesion drops when reward charts, graded work and hierarchical displays are on the walls; it rises when the walls support community and creativity.

In particular, teachers need to beware of the inequity of the 'class reward' chart. A tick chart promising a class party if all children can learn their times tables does *not* create cohesion. Instead, it creates resentment within the class as some students perform the task well and are frustrated by others who do not.

Whether or not school walls have ears, I am quite sure they have a voice which can be heard loud and clear. The physical environment matters; it reflects our identity, shapes our normative behaviours and reflects the values of those who are 'in charge' of the space.

In summary, here are four key points to bear in mind when considering the fostering of contextual wellbeing within the school physical environment.

1. Nature matters: young people thrive when they learn in natural settings and suffer when they are deprived of time outdoors.

2. Comfort and design matter: it is important to set minimum standards for comfort and concentration. Where possible consider natural lighting, low noise levels, flexible seating and warm colours.

3. Ownership matters: all members of a school community thrive when they have been included in the design and creation of the shared physical environment, be it in the design of a new multi-purpose building or the décor in the classroom.

4. Implicit messages have power: you may have good intentions when you put up photos of your school sporting champions but be careful of the underlying message you are giving out. *We need our walls to celebrate rather than adulate.* We need them to support equity, cohesion and community.

CHAPTER TEN

Contextual Wellbeing –
Creating Positive Schools
from the Inside Out

*So how does a school become a positive
school? This chapter introduces a systematic
approach to transforming a school
ethos so that it better supports true and
comprehensive wellbeing. A wellbeing model
is offered that enables schools to move
steadily forward.*

CONTEXTUAL WELLBEING IN SCHOOLS is a state of health, happiness and positive engagement in learning that arises from membership of an equitable, inclusive and cohesive school environment. The contextual wellbeing model offers a concrete usable framework for building contextual wellbeing in your school or college.

Contextual Wellbeing Model

Supporting Wellbeing & SEC in Teachers, School Leaders and Parents

People

Inclusive, Cohesive & Equitable Practice. Focusing on Collaboration, Autonomy & Process

Policy & Practice

Social Norms

Embedding Values in Behaviour. Building Cohesion

Physical Space

Inclusive, Cohesive & Equitable Spaces. Embracing Light, Creativity & Nature

The Contextual Wellbeing model considers the school social context in four distinct domains: people (e.g. staff and students); physical space (e.g. classroom set-up, outdoor spaces); policies and practice (e.g. homework policy, behavioural management practices) and social norms (e.g. whether or not to trust others, how to treat others).

The model recognises that schools are social systems and that all members of the social context of the school are social beings, shaped by their community. People thrive in a healthy school context but struggle in an unhealthy one, no matter how much wellbeing and resiliency training they are given.

The Contextual Wellbeing model is concerned with the development of a school social context which is equitable and supportive of ALL members and thus enables everyone to flourish – academically, socially and emotionally. Contextual Wellbeing is not an add-on program or activity. It is an ongoing process towards building positive, equitable school communities where everyone has the opportunity to flourish.

The following summaries of the domains of Contextual Wellbeing – People, Physical Space, Policy & Practice and Social Norms – bring all these aspects of context together. The table at the end of each summary suggests how each domain looks at both its worst and its best, pictured as a continuum between the negative and positive representation of each area of context. You are invited to consider where your school is currently placed in relation to an ideal vision of each area of contextual wellbeing. Of course, these tables are not exhaustive. You may want to consider other aspects of the four domains that contribute to your own organisation's context and contextual wellbeing.

People

The people in the school community include the school staff, students, parents and allied professionals. All members of a school community impact on the social context in terms of their values, attitudes, skills and expressed behaviours. Attention paid to supporting autonomy, relatedness and competency in both staff and students can help all members of the school community thrive. For example, socially competent staff with manageable levels of stress and high levels of wellbeing will model positive behaviour to their students.

People	Negative Impact	Positive Impact
Teaching staff	Stressed, overwhelmed, poor social and emotional competency (SEC)	Mentally fit, resilient, high self-acceptance, high SEC
Non-Teaching Staff	Stressed, overwhelmed, poor SEC	Mentally fit, resilient, high self-acceptance, high SEC
Students	Disengaged, uninterested in learning, stressed, overwhelmed, poor SEC	Mentally fit, resilient, high self-acceptance, high SEC, motivated, engaged in learning
Parents	Stressed, overwhelmed, poor SEC, over-protective/ negligent	Mentally fit, resilient, high self-acceptance, high SEC, autonomous
Experts	Non-evidence based, fashion followers	Evidence based, valuing creative elaboration, knowledge and experience
Media	Social media in class: unsafe access, unhealthy messages	Access to positive role models, healthy messages, support of face-to-face relationships (rather than 'stranger-friends' on line)

Physical Space

The buildings and grounds of the school and the wider geographical space impacting on the school culture and climate. The classrooms, library and reception, staff room and other rooms; recreational areas such as the canteen and outside areas such as the school oval or playgrounds.

The school physical environment is shaped by people and reflects the norms, values and ideals of the school community, whether openly or covertly. For example, a school gym that displays community photos of students enjoying exercise gives out a very different message to one that features sporting heroes.

Physical Space	Negative Impact	Positive Impact
Classroom furniture	Fixed seating plan Rows of chairs all facing teacher Fixed desks in rows Teacher chair behind front facing desk	Flexible, moving seating plans. Grouped/circular desks alternating with rows Standing options Pedal power desks Teacher with open access to room
Classroom decor	Teacher selected Bare walls, reward charts, accolades, negatively framed messages (e.g. No bullying, no phones, no eating) Rules set by teacher	Student and teacher selected Collaborative Positively framed messages (e.g. this is a supportive environment, quiet area, phone free area) Rules set and signed by class
Hallways and shared space	Non-learning environments Hierarchical symbols such as honours boards Lack of light and colour	Learning spaces with moveable seats and social spaces Community art/ photos Open doors Light and bright

Physical Space	Negative Impact	Positive Impact
Reception	Segregation between adults and students Portrays hierarchical values e.g. trophy cabinets	Open access (all heights!) Light and bright Portrays school values – community, purpose, history of school, etc
School grounds	Segregation A lack of outdoor nature settings	Shared space Multiple 'loose' elements (like wood, pebbles etc) and other evidence of nature that can be embraced by everyone
Beyond the grounds	No nature Busy streets without parking or road crossings Negative advertising	Nature Parking or drop off zones Safe crossings Positive media messages

Policy and Practice

Unlike social norms, policy and practice are overtly known as rules for behaviour. They are the written policies describing the rules of academic, social and emotional management within the school, and the overt practices displayed within the school. However, also unlike social norms, they do not necessarily guide attitudes or the actual behaviour of students. Common policy includes a behavioural management policy and a homework policy. Common practices include the use of rewards in class; award ceremonies; dealing with mobile phone use and practices around the support or reprimanding of students.

Policy and practices shape the level of equity within a school and support a focus on either process or outcomes in learning. They dictate the importance placed on play and creativity and the value placed on competition. For example, a school policy that rejects the use of rewards to motivate students is one that supports intrinsic motivation and equity far more than a policy that rewards the 'top' students and places everyone in a competitive hierarchy.

Policy & Practice	Negative Impact	Positive Impact
Rewards and Awards	Public display of extrinsic rewards and awards for positive social behaviours, academic effort and outcomes Praise used to support compliance	No extrinsic rewards and awards Praise and feedback support autonomy and personal growth Focus on intrinsic motivation and intrinsic rewards
Behavioural management	Punishments/ consequences Zero tolerance No dobbing	Communication, guidance, discussion, bystander intervention, strengths focus
Streaming	In-class and between class streaming from early age	Streaming for upper senior school years only, if at all
Homework	Extensive project-based homework from primary school onwards	No primary school homework
Competition/ collaboration	Forced public competition (e.g. sport carnival, wall chart)	Collaborative learning Competition as choice
Creative opportunity	Structured project Rigid instructions	Free choice, own control, no adult intervention

Social Norms

Social norms are the unwritten rules that guide behaviour within the school community. They also shape attitudes among members of the school community and reflect the strongest values of the school.

Social norms accurately predict student behaviour. They stem from values and develop through repetition. Unhealthy social norms include locking bags and lockers as a sign of mistrust, talking in class and disrespecting teachers and seeing learning as a socially undesirable activity. Healthy social norms include being honest and trustworthy, being respectful to others and viewing engagement with learning as a positive trait.

Healthy norms need to be actively and openly nurtured within the school community. There are two effective ways to do this. In the first case, norms can be set through the establishment of overt rules that are consistently followed through.

Ideally such rules are established with all members of a school community or the relevant subset of that community. Practices that are desirable in class are most easily established with the consensual agreement of all members of the class rather than a directive from the teacher. Still, however well agreed upon and however clearly written down, policy and practice will only become a social norm through regular repetition. It must be reflected in behaviour and re-established if necessary. For example, if a practice of being quiet when the teacher talks is established, it is important that the teacher reminds the class of this rule every time they become overly noisy. If the teacher resorts to shouting at the class to be quiet each time they are noisy, this method will quickly become the social norm over and above any desired policy.

The second way social norms can be established effectively is when they are reflected in other areas of the school context. For

Social Norms	Negative Impact	Positive Impact
Who is admired	Disrespect for teachers and disadvantaged sub-groups of students	Students like and respect teachers and each other Teachers like students and respect school leaders and each other
Behaviour – in class, socially	Emergence of sub-groups; divided aims, hierarchy of social groups	Class operates as a cohesive whole. Students respect each other Students see social groups as different but equal in value Norms and rules within the classroom align
Attitude to learning	Students see learning as overwhelming and/ or irrelevant to 'real life'	Students see learning as engaging, meaningful, relevant, and possible
Honesty and trust	Staff and students exhibit a lack of trust, and a simplistic view of truth and justice	Staff and students demonstrate compassionate honesty and trust within the school community
Value placed on positive education	Staff and students see positive education as irrelevant to real life	Positive education is considered a model for an ideal education and contextual wellbeing
Value placed on school-based activities	Activities are generally viewed as overwhelming, competitive, testing, boring or irrelevant to 'real life'	Activities are viewed as positive, engaging, meaningful, relevant, and inclusive

example, unlocked doors support the establishment of a social norm of honesty far more than locked ones. A hallway that displays pictures from a community event encourages a social norm of valuing relationships far more than a display of award winning work. Look at different areas of context and explore how they do or do not support each other. A healthy school context will have social norms that reflect healthy policy and practice across the whole physical space and all the people in the school community. See table on previous page.

Building Self-determination at the Heart of Contextual Wellbeing

At its core, Contextual Wellbeing supports social cohesion and the process of learning over and above competition and a focus on outcomes. As a general starting point when exploring each contextual domain within your own school, it is useful to ask:

• Is this domain supportive of cohesion and collaboration?

• Is there a focus on process over outcome, with opportunities to embrace progression?

• Is there opportunity to build autonomy and intrinsic motivation?

• Is there equity?

The following diagram presents an overview of the aims of healthy contextual development for the creation of Contextual Wellbeing.

Pathways to Equity

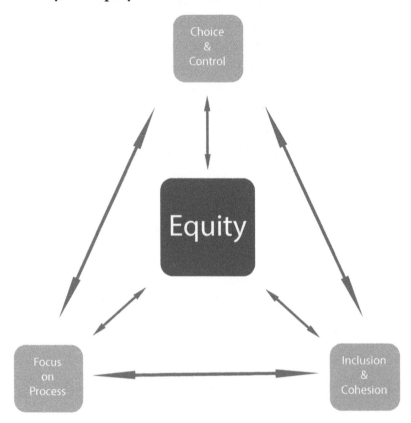

Getting Started – Creating Positive Change

If you want to develop Contextual Wellbeing in your school community or even just in your classroom, then it is a good idea to have a plan of action that incorporates an understanding of the changes you wish to make and the process of change itself.

Change is challenging, even when it is for something we desire. Many of us know it would be a great idea to change our diet so that it was a little healthier, or increase the amount of sleep we get, and yet how many of us manage to achieve these goals? There are reasons why people set the same New Year's resolutions every year – and put them aside after only a few sporadic weeks of progress. Humans feel comfortable living with a sense of familiarity, even if that familiar life is not a desirable one. We struggle to move away from familiarity because it creates temporary disruption and insecurity. It also takes energy and conscious attention to our behaviour. Until our behaviours become ingrained habits, we have to put time and effort into practising them.

Making changes within a school community is no different. It takes time, effort and energy just remembering to do things in a different way. It requires living with a greater degree of uncertainty for a while, as, for instance, with questions about the consequences of change: 'Will a move to being gradeless work out? Will investing time in cohesion building be worth this effort?' It means we may have to reframe our past behaviours as much as challenge our current ones: 'If this new way is better, does this mean I've been getting things wrong until now?'

There is an instrument that is very helpful when it comes to instigating organisational change. Appreciative Inquiry, developed by David Cooperrider in 1986,[1,2,3] offers a philosophy for supporting change from a strengths-based perspective. Its central idea is that the most effective way to create change is to build on what is working within an organisation, as opposed to the more typical focus on changing or removing what is not working.

Traditional approaches to change that focus on 'solving problems' can lead people to feel that they and their organisation are the problem. This in turn can result in them feeling demotivated, despondent and lacking in good will – feelings that are detrimental to the process of successful change.

In support of David Cooperrider's philosophy, my own reviews of literature on goal pursuit and attainment in 2002[4] and in 2012[5] suggest that people are more likely to achieve a goal when they are focused on a positive outcome, rather than when they are trying to move away from an unwanted behaviour. For example, people aiming for better health tend to be more successful than those 'moving away' from unwanted weight. The desired outcome may amount to the same thing, but how you frame the goal makes a big difference to the experience of the journey.

The Appreciative Inquiry model puts people and their relationships at the heart of change management and inspires them to change with a positive vision of 'what can be'. The model has five clear steps: define, discover, dream, design and deliver.

Define – In this first step the topic for change is defined within the organisation. It is important that the definition of the topic is framed in positive terms as opposed to problematic. For example, rather than state that you want to 'rid the school of inequity or reduce competition,' school leaders may decide they want to develop contextual wellbeing or a more equitable environment in their school.

Discover – Participants are invited to identify what is working well or has worked well towards achieving this aim. For example, teachers may talk about the benefits of using public spaces to define school values; the increase in staff morale following a stress management workshop; or the positive reaction of students when brain breaks were introduced. This step may take place in pairs, in small or large groups, or with other activities such as collecting and sharing stories of what went well.

Dream – Members are asked to create a vision which embraces the best possible future for their organisation. This vision may stem from a conversation, a written account or a more visual representation of the future. For example, a school with contextual wellbeing may be envisioned as a school where there are no student hierarchies, where doors are not locked and where everyone manifests intrinsic motivation to learn. Again, discussions may take place between individuals, or in larger groups.

Design – In this step, plans are made to build on the strengths identified in the 'Discover' stage to create the best possible 'Dream' for the future. A working group may be put together to explore the stated policy and practice in the school and look at how to change it in line with the vision for greater contextual wellbeing. Another working group may look at how to use professional development opportunities to better support staff wellbeing, or better support their ability to engage the students in learning.

Deliver – This final step involves the active implementation of the plan. At this stage it is important to keep momentum going with optimum forms of communication. The progress and activities of working groups needs to be communicated regularly, with mentions in the newsletter, on notice boards around the school and at parent forums. John Kotter suggests in the *Harvard Business Review*[6] that leaders should 'walk the talk' and model the vision they wish for their organisation. School leaders can do this by openly expressing support for the school's future vision, rather than scepticism or negativity.

Most people enjoy talking about events that have gone well and enjoy imagining an ideal future, so the philosophy of Appreciative Inquiry actively helps to reduce the anxiety experienced when change is contemplated. People are drawn to a vision of a positive future rather than pushed by fears of deficits and 'the problem'.

This is not to say that there are not problems that need to be addressed in most schools. After all I have spent a good deal of this book talking about contextual 'problems' in schools. But the Appreciative Inquiry approach reframes the way those problems are addressed. David Cooperrider suggests that problems exist because we have a dream for the future that is different from the way things are now. Focusing on the creation of an ideal outcome is a positively focused way of solving existing problems.

Cooperrider's philosophy has supported organisational change around the world, and it can serve as a foundation for planning positive contextual change in your school or college too.

I propose a six-step process that embraces Appreciative Inquiry philosophy while also drawing on other understandings of organisational change. I have added a sixth 'D' to the model – Desire – in the spirit of John Kotter's observation that change rarely occurs unless it is seen as very necessary and highly desirable. Kotter argues that many organisations fail to make positive changes simply because they lack a sense of urgency about making the changes. Desire can create that urgency.

Consider your own health and fitness. You may have a goal to develop an exercise routine. But if you don't really believe that your health, weight and wellbeing will be positively affected by exercise, you are unlikely to make a concerted effort to reach your goal. In contrast, if you do believe your life will be significantly better if you are fitter, or indeed will be significantly diminished if you do not make a change, then you will be highly motivated to invest in a plan. Desire becomes an important ingredient for change.

A Plan of Action for Contextual Wellbeing

Step One: Create DESIRE for change

This includes gathering and gaining information about how and why attention to school context is important, and ways of creating Contextual Wellbeing. This is a good time to have an expert come in and talk to your staff, parents and other stakeholders in your school community, and to hold information-based workshops.

Step Two: DEFINE your subject of change

You may wish to develop Contextual Wellbeing across the whole school or may prefer to begin with a particular class or year group – in which case I suggest you choose from the younger years. You may wish to focus on overall Contextual Wellbeing or on specific ingredients of a positive school context such as equity, cohesion or a change of focus from outcomes to process. Ensure that every planned change is reflected in each of the four domains of context, no matter which one it originates in.

Step Three: DISCOVER what is working in your school

It is important that you involve as many members of the school community as you can in this process. Consider multiple ways in which they can share their experience of what is working well to create a positive school community of equity and cohesion in their classrooms and in the wider school context. You might set up 'What Works Well' boards in the staff room and school reception, hold workshops or focus groups.

If you choose to send out a survey keep it as brief as you can and think carefully about how you are going to explore the ideas and data that come in.

Step Four: DREAM a vision for the future of your school

You can help this process along with a varied approach and inclusion of as many voices as possible. Consider the different ways in which people like to conceptualise their imagined future for the school. Some may like to make a dot point list while others prefer a colourful schematic drawing or mud map. Consider inviting staff to a workshop where they can open up their imaginations and think freely with opportunities for creative expression and brainstorming.

Step Five: DESIGN a plan of action that builds on the information you have collected

Make sure you consider both what you can do and who is going to do it. I recommend you build a step-wise plan to ensure that everyone can experience an ongoing progression and sense of achievement across the school. For example, if you want to become a 'grade free' primary school (with the exception of mandatory grades on reports), you may decide to start with a simplification of grades in term one or begin by letting students suggest their own grades for their work.

Step SIX: DELIVER your plan of action

Roll up your sleeves and begin to put your changes in place, using as many opportunities to communicate plans and changes as you can. Again, make sure that every change is reflected in all domains of context, no matter which one it originates from. For example, if you want to create a growth mindset as a social norm, make sure your staff understand exactly what a growth mindset is and how to support its development; ensure that policy and practice exhibits a clear focus on process rather than grades and awards, and take note of any conflicting messages given out by the physical environment.

It is important to view the delivery process as circular rather than linear. You can do this by providing constant feedback on what is happening and what is working. Also, revisit the plan from step one onwards at regular intervals – I suggest at least once every six months.

Using Appreciative Inquiry to Create Contextual Wellbeing in Your School

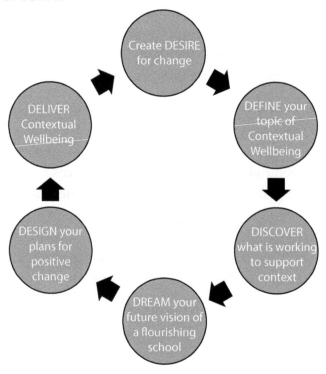

It has often been said that it takes a whole village to raise a child. I certainly believe it takes a whole healthy school context to help a child to flourish. With passion, careful planning and perseverance, great things develop.

Contextual Wellbeing matters because every child matters.

References

CHAPTER ONE

1. Seligman, M. E. P. (2002). *Authentic happiness: Using the new positive psychology to realize your potential for lasting fulfillment.* NY: Free Press.
2. Seligman, M. E. P. (2011). *Flourishing.* NY: Free Press.
3. Campbell, Joseph (1988). Interview with Bill Moyers, *The Power of Myth* (New York), 30.
4. Campbell, J. (1993). *Myths to Live By.* NY: Penguin.
5. Csikszentmihalyi, M (1990). *Flow: The Psychology of Optimal Experience.* NY: Harper & Row.
6. Dick, P. K. (1968). *Do Androids Dream of Electric Sheep?* UK: Doubleday.
7. Deci, E. L. & Ryan, R. M. (1985). *Intrinsic Motivation and Self-determination in Human Behavior.* NY: Plenum.
8. Deci, E. L. & Ryan, R. M. (1987). The support of autonomy and the control of behaviour. *Journal of Personality and Social Psychology*, 53(6), 1024–37.

CHAPTER TWO

1. McGrath, Michael (2016). Nancy Reagan and the negative impact of the 'Just Say No' anti-drug campaign. The Guardian

Online Wed March 9. Retrieved from https://www.theguardian.com/society/2016/mar/08/nancy-reagan-drugs-just-say-no-dare-program-opioid-epidemic

2. Newton, J. (1993). As DARE grows, so does controversy: Youth: Despite critics, the anti-drug program expands nationally in its 10th year. But some see support fall in LAPD. Los Angeles Times Sep 9. 1993. Retrieved from http://articles.latimes.com/1993-09-09/news/mn-33235_1_anti-drug-program

3. Wysong, E. & Wright, D. W. (1995). A decade of DARE: efficacy, politics and drug education. *Sociological Focus*, 28(3).

4. Bronson, P. & Merryman, A, (2009). *Nurture Shock: Why Everything We Think about Raising our Children is Wrong*. Reading, UK: Cox & Wyman.

5. West, S. L. & O'Neal, K. K. (2004). Project D.A.R.E. outcome effectiveness revisited. *American Journal of Public Health*, 94(6), 1027–9.

6. Weissbourd, R., (1996). The feel-good trap (self-esteem movement in education). *New Republic*, 215(8–9), 12–15.

7. Branden, N. (1969). *The Psychology of Self-Esteem*. US: Bantam Books.

8. Cowen, E. L., Hightower, A. D., Pedro-Carroll, J. L., Work, W. C., Wyman, P. A. & Haffey, W. G. (1996). School-based prevention for children at risk. The Primary Mental Health Project. Washington, DC: American Psychological Association.
Cowen, E. L., Izzo, L. D., Miles, H., Telschow, E. F., Trost, M. A. & Zax, M. (1963). A preventive mental health program in the school setting: Description and evaluation. *Journal of Psychology*, 56, 307–56.

9. Kane, R., Thomson, T., Roberts, Clare., Bishop, Brian. (2003). The prevention of depressive symptoms in rural school children: A randomized controlled trial. *Journal of Consulting and Clinical Psychology*, 71(3), 622–8.

10. Pattison, C. & Lynd-Stevenson, R. M. (2001). The prevention of depressive symptoms in children: The immediate and long-term outcomes of a school-based program. *Behaviour Change*, 18(2), 92–102.

11. Layard, R. (2003). Happiness – Has Social Science a Clue? [Lionel Robbins Memorial Lectures 2002/3]. London School of Economics and Political Science.

12. Huppert, F., Baylis, N. & Keverne, B. (2004). *The Science of Well-Being*. Oxford, UK: Oxford University Press.

13. Weare, K. & Nind, M. (2011). Mental health promotion and problem prevention in schools: What does the evidence say? *Health Promotion International*, 26(S1).

14. Ecclestone, K. (2015). Well-being programmes in schools might be doing children more harm than good. The Conversation. Retrieved from https://theconversation.com/well-being-programmes-in-schools-might-be-doing-children-more-harm-than-good-36573

15. Greenberg, M. T., Domitrovich, C. and Bumbarger, B. (2001). Preventing Mental Disorders in School Aged Children. A Review of the Effectiveness of Prevention Programmes. Prevention Research Center for the Promotion of Human Development, College of Health and Human Development, Pennsylvania State University.

16. Huppert, F. A., Marks, N., Clark, A., Siegrist, J., Stuter, A., Vitterso, J. & Wahrendorf, M. (2009). Measuring well-being across Europe: Description of the ESS well-being module and preliminary findings. *Social Indicator Research*, 91, 301–15.

17. Norrish, J. (ed). (2015). *Positive Education: The Geelong Grammar School Journey*. NY: Oxford University Press.

18. Wells, J., Barlow, J. and Stewart-Brown, S. (2003). A systematic review of universal approaches to mental health promotion in schools. *Health Educ*ation, 103, 197–220.

19. Weare, K. & Nind, M. (2011). Mental health promotion and problem prevention in schools: What does the evidence say? *Health Promotion International*, 26(S1).

20. Burns & Street (2003). *Standing Without Shoes*, Penguin Australia.

21. Burns, G. W. (2016). personal correspondence with Helen Street, 10 March 2016.

22. Mercer, S., McMillen, J. & DeRosier, M. (2009). Predicting change in children's aggression and victimization using classroom-level descriptive norms of aggression and pro-social behaviour. *Journal of School Psychology*, 47, 267–89.

CHAPTER THREE

1. Australian Bureau of Statistics (2012). Profiles of Health, Australia, 2011–13. Retrieved from http://www.abs.gov.au/ausstats/abs@.nsf/Lookup/4338.0main+features42011-13

2. Australian Bureau of Statistics (2015). National Health Survey, 2014–15. Retrieved from http://www.abs.gov.au/ausstats/abs@.nsf/Lookup/by%20Subject/4364.0.55.001~2014-15~Main%20Features~Psychological%20distress~16

3. Sawyer, M. G., Arney, F. M., Baghurst, P., Clark, J. J., Graetz, B. W., Kosky, R. J., Nurcombe, B., Patton, G. C., Prior, M. R., Raphael, B., Rey, J. M., Whaites, L. C. & Zubrick, S. R. (2001). The mental health of young people in Australia: key findings from the child and adolescent component of the national survey of mental health and wellbeing. *Australian and New Zealand Journal of Psychiatry*, 35, 806–14.

4. Mission Australia (2018). The 2017 Mission Australia Youth Survey. Retrieved from https://www.missionaustralia.com.au/publications/annual-reports/annual-report-2017

5. Hattie, John (2014). BBC Radio 4: The Educators. Interview with Sarah Montague, first *broadcast: 20 August 2014*. Retrieved

fromhttps://visible-learning.org/2014/09/john-hattie-interview-bbc-radio-4/

CHAPTER FOUR

1. Xueqin, J. (2010). The Test Chinese Schools Still Fail. *Wall Street Journal* (8 December). Retrieved from https://www.wsj.com/articles/SB100014240527487037667045760086924930386

2. Gray, Peter (2011). The Decline of Play and the Rise of Psychopathology in Children and Adolescents. American Journal of Play, 3(4), 443–63.

3. Whitebread, D. (2012). The Importance of Play: a report on the value of children's play with a series of policy recommendations. TIE, April.

4. Gupta, A. (2009). Vygotskian perspectives on using dramatic play to enhance children's development and balance creativity with structure in the early childhood classroom. *Early Child Development and Care*, 179(8), 1041–54.

5. Robinson, K. (1999). All our futures: Creativity, culture, and education. Report to the National Advisory Committee on Creative and Cultural Education. London: National Advisory Committee on Creative & Cultural Education.

6. Robinson, K. (2011). *Out of our minds: Learning to be creative.* Oxford: Capstone.

7. Whitebread, D. (2014). Hard Evidence: at what age are children ready for school? The Conversation https://theconversation.com/hard-evidence-at-what-age-are-children-ready-for-school-29005

8. Whitebread, D. & Jarvis, P. (2010). Too much too soon: Reflection upon the school starting age. Retrieved from http://www.toomuchtoosoon.org/uploads/2/0/3/8/20381265/scm_submission_-_school_starting_age_.pdf

9. Gray, P. (2013). *Free to learn: Why unleashing the instinct to play will make our children happier, more self-reliant, and better students for life.* NY: Basic Books.

10. Roenneberg, T., Kuehnle, T., Pramstaller, P., Ricken, J., Havel, M., Guth, A. & Merrow, M., (2004). Marker For the End of Adolescence. *Current Biology*, 14(24), 38–9.

11. Kirby, M., Maggi, S. & D'Angiulli, A. (2011). School start times and the sleep–wake cycle of adolescents: a review and critical evaluation of available evidence. *Educational Researcher*, 40(2), 56–61.

12. Jensen, E. (2000). Moving with the brain in mind. *Educational Leadership*, 58(3), 34–8.

13. McInnes, K., Howard, J., Miles, G. & Crowley, K. (2011). Differences in practitioners' understanding of play and how this influences pedagogy and children's perceptions of play. *Early Years*, 31(2), 121–33.

14. Victorian Department of Education (2014). Parliament of Victoria Education and Training Committee. Inquiry into the approaches to homework in Victorian schools. Retrieved from https://www.parliament.vic.gov.au/file_uploads/ETC_Homework_Inquiry_final_report_PWkrPPVH.pdf

15. Canadian Council on Learning (2009). A systematic review of literature examining the impact of homework on academic achievement. Retrieved from http://edu.au.dk/fileadmin/edu/Udgivelser/SystematicReview_HomeworkApril27-2009.pdf

16. Victorian Department of Education (2014). Parliament of Victoria Education and Training Committee. Inquiry into the approaches to homework in Victorian schools. Retrieved from https://www.parliament.vic.gov.au/file_uploads/ETC_Homework_Inquiry_final_report_PWkrPPVH.pdf

17. Katz, I., Buzukashvili, T. and Feingold, L. (2012). Homework Stress: Construct Validation of a Measure. *Journal of Experimental Education*, 80(4), 405–21.

18. Rønning, Marte (2011). Who benefits from homework assignments? Economics of Education Review, 30(1), 55–64.

19. Huffington Post, unnamed author (2012). François Hollande, French President, pledges to abolish homework as part of education reforms. 15 October. Retrieved from https://www.huffingtonpost.com/2012/10/12/french-president-francois_n_1962494.html

20. Sage, Adam (2017). French children are promised an end to homework. The Times: Paris, 9 June. Retrieved from https://www.thetimes.co.uk/article/french-children-are-promised-an-end-to-homework-25wbcjwzp

21. Blume, Howard (2011). Less stress if the dog eats it – In new L.A. unified policy, homework will count for just 10% of a student's grade. 27 June, Los Angeles Times.

22. Kralovec, Etta (2014). Should schools ban homework? CNN. Retrieved from http://edition.cnn.com/2014/09/05/opinion/kralovec-ban-homework/index.html

23. Schachter, Ron (2005). The End of Recess. District Administration, August. Retrieved from https://www.districtadministration.com/article/end-recess

24. Walker, Timothy D. (2014). How Finland Keeps Kids Focused through Free Play. Atlantic Daily, 30 June. Retrieved from https://www.theatlantic.com/education/archive/2014/06/how-finland-keeps-kids-focused/373544/

25. Turner, Janice (2017). Learning to Chill. Weekend Australian Magazine, 27–28 May.

26. Cook, Henrietta (2017). 'Ready to go': School keeps kids switched on by ending each hour with Finnish break. The Age, 17 October.

27. Sahlberg, Pasi (2017). FinnishED Leadership: Four Big, Inexpensive Ideas to Transform Education (Corwin Impact Leadership Series).

28. OECD (2017). PISA 2015 Results in Focus. Retrieved from http://www.oecd.org/pisa/pisa-2015-results-in-focus.pdf

29. OECD (2017). PISA 2015 Results (Volume III): Students' Well-Being, PISA, OECD Publishing, Paris. Retrieved from http://dx.doi.org/10.1787/9789264273856-en

CHAPTER FIVE

1. Adler, R. B. & Rodman, G. (1997). *Understanding Human Communication*. UK: Harcourt Brace, 327–329.

2. Carron, Albert V. & Brawley, Lawrence, R. (2000). Cohesion. *Small Group Research*, 31(1), 89–106.

3. Pengelley, Richard (2017). Cost of Excellence in Childhood (Positive Schools Hong Kong 2017). The Positive Times. Retrieved from http://positivetimes.com.au/cost-of-excellence-in-childhood-by-richard-pengelley-hong-kong-2017/

4. Street, H. (2002). Exploring relationships between goal setting, goal pursuit and depression: A review. *Australian Psychologist*, 37(2), 95–103.

5. Street, H. (2012). Goals and Goalsetting: Prevention and Treatment of Depression. In *Encyclopedia of the Sciences of Learning*, ed. Norbert M. Seel. US: Springer.

6. Duckworth, Angela (2017). *Grit: Why Passion and Resilience are the Secrets to Success*. London: Vermilion.

7. Bott, D. (2017). Applying the Science of Achievement. The Positive Times. Retrieved from http://positivetimes.com.au/applying-the-science-of-achievement-david-bott-geelong-grammar-ps17/

8. Seligman, Martin & Peterson, Christopher (2004). Character Strengths and Virtues. *American Psychological Association*, Oxford University Press.

9. Weingarten, G. (2007). Pearls Before Breakfast: Can one of the nation's great musicians cut through the fog of a D.C. rush hour? Let's find out. *Washington Post*, 8 April.

10. Johnston, O. & Wildy, H. (2016). The effects of streaming in the secondary school on learning outcomes for Australian students – A review of the international literature. *Australian Journal of Education*, 60(1), 42–59.

11. Chorzempa, B. F. & Graham, S. (2006). Primary grade teachers' use of within-class ability grouping in reading. *Journal of Educational Psychology*, 98(3), 529–42.

12. Butler, R. (2008). Ego-involving and frame of reference effects of tracking on elementary school students' motivational orientations and help seeking in math class. *Social Psychology of Education*, 11(1), 5–34.

13. Smyth, Emer & McCoy, Selina (2011). Improving Second-Level Education: Using Evidence for Policy Development. Economic and Social Research Institute. Renewal Series: Paper 5.

CHAPTER SIX

1. Street, H. (2010). The why not the what: the positive power of intrinsic motivations in client goal setting and pursuit in Burns, G. (ed.). *Happiness, Healing Enhancement: your casebook collection for using positive psychology in therapy*. Hoboken, NJ: John Wiley & Sons.

2. Kohn, A. (1999). *Punished by Rewards*. New York, NY: Houghton Mifflin Co.

3. Deci, E. L. & Ryan, R. M. (2000). The 'what' and 'why' of goal pursuits: Human needs and the self-determination of behavior. *Psychological Inquiry*, 11(4), 227–68.

4. Street, Helen (2017). Motivation outside in, inside out. In Slemp, G., Murray, S. & White, M. (eds). *Future Directions in Well-being: Education, Organizations, and Policy.* Springer.

5. Street, H. & Porter, N. (eds). (2014). *Better Than OK: Helping Young People to Flourish at School and Beyond.* Fremantle, WA: Fremantle Press.

6. Kohn, A. (1999). Punished by Rewards. New York, NY: Houghton Mifflin Co.

CHAPTER SEVEN

1. Adler, R. B. & Rodman, G. (1997). *Understanding Human Communication.* UK: Harcourt Brace, 327–9.

2. Beal, Daniel J., Cohen, Robin R., Burke, Michael J., Mclendon, Christy L., Zedeck, Sheldon (ed). (2003). Cohesion and Performance in Groups: A Meta-Analytic Clarification of Construct Relations. *Journal of Applied Psychology,* 88(6), 989–1004.

3. Adler, R. B. & Rodman, G. (1997). Understanding Human Communication. UK: Harcourt Brace, 327–9.

4. Bruhn, J .G. (2009). The Concept of Social Cohesion, in *The Group Effect.* Springer Science+Business Media, 30–48.

5. Street, Helen (2016). The importance of classroom 'glue'. *Western Teacher,* 45(1), 28.

6. Battistich, V. & Hom, A. (1997). The relationship between students' sense of their school as a community and their involvement in problem behaviors. *American Journal of Public Health,* 87(12), 1997–2001.

7. Deci, E. L. & Ryan, R. M. (1985). Intrinsic Motivation and Self-determination in Human Behavior. NY: Plenum.

8. Keyes, C. L. M. (2009). The nature and importance of positive mental health in America's adolescents. In R. Gilman, E. S.

Huebner & M. J. Furlong (eds), *Handbook of positive psychology in schools*. NY: Routledge, 9–23.

9. Meyers, J. & Meyers, B. (2003). Bi-directional influences between positive psychology and primary prevention. *School Psychology Quarterly*, 18(2), 222–9.

10. Kameda, T., Takezawa, M. & Hastie, R. (2005). Where do social norms come from? The example of communal sharing. *Current Directions in Psychological Science*, 14(6), 331–4.

11. Bicchieri, C. (2006). *The Grammar of Society: the Nature and Dynamics of Social Norms,* NY: Cambridge University Press.

12. Behavioural Insights Team (2012). Applying behavioural insights to reduce fraud, error and debt. Cabinet Office Behavioural Insights Team, UK.

13. Street, H. (2004). Childhood wellbeing in the classroom: the importance of a nurturing environment, in Smith, L. & Riley, D. (eds). *Checking the Pulse*. Armidale, Australia: ACEL/ACE.

14. Street, Helen (2016). Pathways to Creativity, in Robinson, Paula (ed). *Practising Positive Education: A Guide to Improving Wellbeing Literacy in Schools*. PPI &Knox Grammar School, NSW, Australia.

15. Street, Helen (2017). Measures of success: Exploring the importance of context in the delivery of wellbeing and social and emotional learning programs in Australian primary and secondary schools, in Frydenberg, E. Martin, A. J. and Collie R. J. (eds). *Social and Emotional Learning in Australia and the Asia Pacific*. Singapore: Springer Science and Business.

16. Ariely, Dan (2012). *The Honest Truth about Dishonesty*. US: Harper Collins.

17. Street, Helen (2017). Why Honesty Matters, in The Positive Times. Retrieved from http://positivetimes.com.au/why-honesty-matters-by-dr-helen-street-ps17/

18. Sathyanarayana, R. (2013). Schools in Tamil Nadu Promote Honesty Shops. *Deccan Herald*, 19 October.

CHAPTER EIGHT

1. Cahill, H., Shaw, G., Wynn, J. & Smith, G. (2004). Translating Caring into Action: an Evaluation of the Victorian Catholic Education Welfare Professional Development Initiative. Australian Youth Research Centre, University of Melbourne.
2. Street, H. (2004). Childhood wellbeing in the classroom: the importance of a nurturing environment, in Smith, L. & Riley, D. (eds). *Checking the Pulse*. Armidale, Australia: ACEL/ACE.
3. Street, H., Muliadi, F. & Porter, N. (2015). Voices for Living Project: The Positive Schools Initiative, in The Positive Times. Retrieved from http://positivetimes.com.au/wp-content/uploads/2015/10/Voices-for-Living-Project.pdf
4. Fuller, Andrew & Hendry, John (2018). The Resilient Mindset. Retrieved from http://andrewfuller.com.au
5. Fuller, Andrew & Wicking, Andrew (2015). Pathways to Resilience: Resilient Youth Australia, September. Retrieved from http://andrewfuller.com.au/wp-content/uploads/2016/02/ResiliencePathways.pdf
6. Fuller, Andrew & Wicking, Andrew (2014). Retrieved from http://andrewfuller.com.au/resilience-an-update/
7. Cole, D. A. L., Howard, D. L. & George, S. (1987). Construct validity and the relation between depression and social skill. *Journal of Counseling Psychology*, 34(3), 315–21.
8. Danielsen, A. G., Samdal, O., Hetland, J. & Wold, B. (2009). School related social support and students' perceived life satisfaction. *Journal of Educational Research*, 102, 303–20.
9. Roffey, Sue (2014). *Circle Solutions for Student Wellbeing*. Sage Publications.

10. Heron, Steve (2015). BUZ (Build Up Zone). Nurture Works Foundation. Retrieved from http://www.buildupzone.com/

11. Carr-Gregg, Michael (2007). *Real Wired Child: What Parents Need to Know about Kids Online*. Penguin Australia.

12. Roffey, S. (2012). Pupil wellbeing – teacher wellbeing: Two sides of the same coin? *Educational & Child Psychology*, 29(4), 8–17.

13. Collie, R. J. (2017). Teachers' Social and Emotional Competence: Links with Social and Emotional Learning and Positive Workplace Outcomes in Australian primary and secondary schools. In Frydenberg, E., Martin, A. J. and Collie R. J. (eds). *Social and Emotional Learning in Australia and the Asia Pacific*. Singapore: Springer Science and Business.

14. Spilt, Jantine L., Koomen, Helma M. Y. & Thijs, Jochem T. (2011). Teacher Wellbeing: The Importance of Teacher–Student Relationships. *Educational Psychology Review*, 23, 457–77.

15. Kyriacou, C. (2011). Teacher stress: From prevalence to resilience. In J. Langan-Fox & C. L. Cooper, *Handbook of stress in the occupations*. Northampton, MA: Edward Elgar Publishing, 161–73.

16. Markow, D., Macia, L. & Lee, H. (2013). The MetLife survey of the American teacher: Challenges for school leadership. NY: Metropolitan Life Insurance Company.

17. Cody, Anthony (2014). John Thompson: Gallup Poll Finds Majority of Teachers 'Not Engaged'. *Education Week Australia*, 16 April. Retrieved from http://blogs.edweek.org/teachers/living-in-dialogue/2014/04/john_thompson_gallup_poll_find.html

18. Greenberg M. T., Brown J. L. and Abenavoli R. M. (2016). Teacher stress and health effects on teachers, students, and schools [Issue brief]. Retrieved from http://http://www.rwjf.org/content/dam/farm/reports/issue_briefs/2016/rwjf430428

19. Milkie, Melissa A. & Warner, Catharine H. (2011). Classroom Learning Environments and the Mental Health of First Grade Children. *Journal of Health and Social Behavior*, 52(1), 4–22.

20. Oberle, Eva & Schonert-Reichl, Kimberly A. (2016). Stress contagion in the classroom? The link between classroom teacher burnout and morning cortisol in elementary school students. *Social Science & Medicine*, 159, 30–37.

21. Duffy, Gavin & Elwood, Jannette (2013). The Perspectives of 'disengaged' Students in the 14–19 Phase on motivations and Barriers to Learning within the Contexts of Institutions and Classrooms. *London Review of Education*, 11(2): 112–26.

22. Wang, Ming-Te, Brinkworth, Maureen & Eccles, Jacquelynne (2013). Moderating Effects of Teacher-Student Relationship in Adolescent Trajectories of Emotional and Behavioral Adjustment. *Developmental Psychology*, 49(4), 690–705.

23. Humphrey, N., Lendrum, A. & Wigelsworth, M. (2010). Social and Emotional Aspects of Learning (SEAL) in Secondary Schools: National Evaluation Research Report DFE-RR049. UK: Department for Education.

24. Street, H. (2011). Life Overload: Immediate Life-Saving Strategies from a Stress Expert. Sydney: Finch Publishing.

25. Quinn, Cathy (2017). Strengths Based Approach to Parents for Schools. The Positive Times. http://positivetimes.com.au/1319-2/

CHAPTER NINE

1. Phillips, Mark (2014). *A Place for Learning: The Physical Environment of Classrooms*. Edutopia.

2. Campbell, Joseph (1988). Interview with Bill Moyers, *The Power of Myth* (New York), 30.

3. Earthman, Glen I. (1997). *The Relationship Between School Buildings, Student Achievement and Behavior*. PEB Exchange. Paris, France: OECD, January.

4. Langer, Ellen (2009). *Counterclockwise: Mindful Health and the Power of Possibility*. US: Ballantine Books.

5. Higgins, Steve, Elaine Hall, Kate Wall, Pam Woolner & Caroline McCaughey (2005). The Impact of School Environments: A literature review produced for the Design Council. Centre for Learning and Teaching, School of Education, Communication and Language Science, University of Newcastle, UK.

6. Moss, Stephen (2012). *Natural Childhood*. UK: National Trust.

7. Kellert, Stephen (2015). Build nature into education. *Nature*, 523(7560), 288–9.

8. Louv, R. (2005). *Last Child in the Woods: Saving Our Children from Nature-Deficit Disorder*, Algonquin Books, Chapel Hill.

9. Moss, Stephen (2012). *Natural Childhood*. UK: National Trust.

10. Pagels, Peter, Anders Raustorp, Antonio Ponce De Leon, Fredrika Mårtensson & Cecilia Boldemann (2014). A repeated measurement study investigating the impact of school outdoor environment upon physical activity across ages and seasons in Swedish second, fifth and eighth graders. *BMC Public Health*, 14, 803.

11. Sigman, A. (2007). Agricultural Literacy: Giving concrete children food for thought. Retrieved from www.face-online.org.uk/resources/news/Agricultural%20Literacy.pdf

12. OFSTED (2008). Learning outside the classroom: how far should you go? Manchester: Office for Standards in Education, Children's Services and Skills. Retrieved from www.ofsted.gov.uk/news/report-highlights-benefit-of-learning-outside-classroom Quoted in RSPB (2010). Every Child Outdoors.

13. Dickie, Ian, Ece Ozdermiroglu & Zara Phang (2011). Assessing the Benefits of Learning Outside the Classroom in Natural Environments. London: EFTEC. Retrieved from www.eftec.co.uk/

14. Dillon, J., Morris, M., O'Donnell, L., Reid, A., Rickinson, M. & Scott, W. (2004). Engaging and Learning with the Outdoors: the Final Report of the Outdoor Classroom in a Rural Context. Action Research Project. Slough: NFER.

15. Christie, Beth, Simon Beames, Peter Higgins, Robbie Nicol & Hamish Ross (2014). Outdoor Learning provision in Scottish Schools. *Scottish Educational Review*, 46(1), 48–64.

16. Cosco, N. (2005). Environmental Interventions for Healthy Development of Young Children in the Outdoors. Open Space, People Space Conference, 19–21 September 2007, Edinburgh. Retrieved from www.openspace.eca.ac.uk/conference/proceedings/PDF/Cosco.Pdf

17. Higgins, Steve, Elaine Hall, Kate Wall, Pam Woolner & Caroline McCaughey (2005). The Impact of School Environments: A literature review produced for the Design Council. Centre for Learning and Teaching, School of Education, Communication and Language Science, University of Newcastle, UK.

18. Karpen, D. (1993). Full Spectrum Polarized Lighting: An Option for Light Therapy Boxes. 101st Annual Convention of the American Psychological Association, Toronto.

19. Earthman, G. I. (2004). Prioritization of 31 Criteria for School Building Adequacy. Retrieved from http://www.aclu-md.org/facilities_report.pdf

20. Fisher, K. (2001). Building Better Outcomes: The impact of school infrastructure on student outcomes and behaviour. Department of Education, Training and Youth Affairs, Australia.

21. Knight, G. & Noyes, J. (1999). Children's Behaviour and the Design of School Furniture. *Ergonomics* 42(5), 747–60.

22. Burke, C. & Grosvenor, I. (2003). *The School I'd Like*. Routledge.

23. Sommer, Robert (1977). Classroom Layout. *Theory into Practice*, 16(3), 174–5.

24. Van Den Berg, Yvonne H. M. & Cillessen, Antonius H. N. (2015). Peer status and classroom seating arrangements: A social relations analysis. *Journal of Experimental Child Psychology*, 130(16), 19.

CHAPTER TEN

1. Cooperrider, D. L. (1986). Appreciative Inquiry: Toward a Methodology for Understanding and Enhancing Organizational Innovation. Unpublished Doctoral Dissertation, Case Western Reserve University, Cleveland, Ohio. contact: 1-216-368-2055 or 1-216-368-2215.

2. Cooperrider, David L. & Srivastva, Suresh (1987). Appreciative Inquiry in Organizational Life. *Organizational Change and Development*, 1, 129–69.

3. Cooperrider, D. L. (1995). Introduction to Appreciative Inquiry. In W. French & C. Bell (eds), *Organization Development* (5th edn). Prentice Hall.

4. Street, H. (2002). Exploring relationships between goal setting, goal pursuit and depression: A review. *Australian Psychologist*, 37(2), 95–103.

5. Street, H. (2012). Goals and Goalsetting: Prevention and Treatment of Depression. In *Encyclopedia of the Sciences of Learning* (ed) Norbert M. Seel. US: Springer.

6. Kotter, John P. (2007). *Leading Change: Why Transformation Efforts Fail*. Harvard Business Review. January.

About Helen

Helen is an honorary Associate Professor in the Graduate School of Education at the University of Western Australia.

Since gaining her PhD in applied social psychology in 1998 in the UK, Helen has conducted research, presented at conferences and in schools around the world, and has written four books, several book chapters and more than 100 articles and academic papers. Her first book *Standing Without Shoes* was co-written with George Burns in 2003 and includes a foreword by His Holiness the Dalai Lama.

In 2009, Helen founded the Positive Schools Initiative (PSI) with Neil Porter. The Positive Schools Initiative supports solution focused, evidence-based ideas and strategies to improve youth mental health and wellbeing. The PSI features the highly acclaimed Positive Schools Conferences which are held across Australia and SE Asia each year. The Positive Schools conferences have become known as world premier mental health and wellbeing events for teachers and have resulted in significant development in school-based wellbeing practices at an international level. Helen presents regularly at Positive Schools in addition to creating and chairing every event with Neil.

Helen and Neil also established and edit *The Positive Times*, a free online magazine for teachers which features articles and presentation notes from Positive Schools presenters.

In addition, Helen is a consultant with the West Australian Health Department and the West Australian Association of Mental Health, and appears regularly on TV and radio. As a powerful advocate for the creation of positive school communities, she is particularly interested in the development of positive school contexts in which young people can develop intrinsic motivation, self-determination and life-long wellbeing.

Helen believes that students will flourish when, and only when, they feel connected to a healthy school context.

Her work has been adopted by schools in Europe, Asia and Australia.

www.contextualwellbeing.com.au
@drhelenstreet
www.positiveschools.com.au
www.positiveschools.asia
www.positivetimes.com.au

Lightning Source UK Ltd.
Milton Keynes UK
UKHW021811061218
333570UK00003B/315/P